Words on *K*

Rhys Stenner has been a b
me in the time I have kno\ , ... p........... .u. Christ
and Wales is infectious. Time is one of the great things
you can give someone. Rhys and his family have
travelled for many years and helped build relationships
beyond human imagination. We both play under the
best coach that is Jesus Christ, me a "piano pusher",
Rhys a "piano player", and I as a former forward still
getting things wrong at times. I am blessed to call him
my friend and Brother in Christ.

> *Garin Jenkins, Welsh rugby international, 58 caps,*
> *played in three world cups 1991-1999, five nations*
> *champions 1994, played in Wales first ever win v*
> *South Africa 1999, BBC commentator*

It began with a desire to let passion drive ministry. Rhys
had a passion for Welsh rugby and things Welsh and he
wanted to give it expression. First he invited a handful
of men to drive from Brighton to Cardiff to watch Wales
play. Then Eleven of us were asked if we would join him
for a one off weekend mission to the Rhondda and
Merthyr valleys. That began a relationship with the
people and valleys of Wales that has grown and
matured and continues for me and many others.

> *Phillip Deuk, Brighton*

My recollection is that Rhys and Philip wrote to a
number of fellowships in Wales offering help and
apparently we were the only ones who replied (we were
impressed with your granddad`s Welsh cap). You

promised to come over to help us. I think there were 10-12 people on the first visit: yourself, Philip, Rowland, Mike and Sarah Bray, and a few others. What impressed us was that you did exactly as you promised: you came alongside us, encouraged us and then returned home. Then returned the next year and the next, right up to the present day.

We are especially thrilled that you are going in to Aberfan this year, almost a culmination of your commitment to us in this area. You and your family and your church family are very precious and special to us here in Troedyrhiw. It has been a privilege for us here in the village to have been part of such a move of God. Thank you for involving us in such a move of the Holy Spirit.

> *David and Jean Chilcott, Pastor of Tabernacle, Troederhiw*

I first met Rhys 3 years ago when he and the New Hope Baptist choir were on a mission in Wales.

Jacob my son, had been asked to sing a solo for the congregation. Rhys immediately made us feel welcome and it was obvious from the start that he had a passion for the Welsh and that it was his calling to see a revival in the Christian faith here in Wales. The evening was a complete success when many of the congregation were moved to tears and giving their lives to Christ. This was the first of many such nights that I have attended with Rhys and the choir and I am still taken aback as to how moving and spiritual these events are. I am also humbled that the choir members give up their holidays and their time to come over to Wales to spread the Gospel. Their presence here in Wales is making a difference in people's lives. Since our first meeting Rhys and I have become firm friends who continues to encourage me in the Gospel. We have met up on many occasions here in Wales and with other rugby players with a view of using rugby as a vehicle to spread the Word. In Easter 2016, we came to Atlanta, where I was humbled to be inaugurated into the New Hope Baptist Hall of Fame. I have found Rhys to be a genuine honest man whose passion and energy to spread the Gospel knows no end. I as a Welshman am so pleased and privileged that he has a special place for Wales in his heart and that his enthusiasm to see a spiritual revival in Wales will benefit so many people in years to come.

Emyr Lewis, Welsh rugby international, 41 caps, five nations champions 1994, defeated World Champions Australia with club Llanelli 1992, commentator BBC Radio Cymru.

Rhys Stenner was among a group of young people in Teignmouth who came to personal faith in Christ at a time when the church was experiencing growth and transformation. Every part of the church's life and witness was marked by the confident sharing of what God had given in Christ because of His love for the world. Some would call it a revival. In 1987 I was called to serve through the Baptist Union of Wales in a new and experimental role of encouraging and assisting churches in their witness to Christ. Two experiences stand out from a visit made by Rhys and Louise at that time. Going together to Llanelli to watch the All Blacks. The weather was atrocious. Fierce winds and driving, bitterly cold, horizontal rain, and the match curtailed, along with police safety advice to the passionate crowd. Going to Blaengarw to meet Mrs. Charles, the secretary of the decaying but once magnificent Bethania Chapel, to hear the story, and glimpse a little of the challenges faced. I had no idea that Rhys would find in his heart such a powerful and persistent call to return again and again to Wales to help, and the story, which is still unfolding, is remarkable.

> *Rev Ian Burley, 40 years pastoral experience*
> *including years in Wales, Rhys Stenner's first pastor*
> *in Teignmouth, and still a mentor today.*

Rhys Stenner has a contagious passion for Welsh rugby. Even an American like myself can't help being drawn into the game when Rhys tells the story. What makes him so articulate about this sport? Maybe it's his encyclopedic memory of past players and matches, or his relationships with present players and coaches of note, or even his love for the culture of the stadium; songs and all. It is surely all of these but I believe it is deeper. Rugby has a place in Rhys' soul, and those seeds were planted by a Grandfather who played for Wales. The stuff of life and matters of faith are often illustrated on the sports field, and Rhys has a marvelous ability to use a story to communicate and encourage. I know I love to "hear" him, and know you will too.

> *John Conrad, Associate Minister and Director of the*
> *New Hope Choir.*

I met Pastor Rhys Stenner in 2010 after being contacted via Philip Deuk. We were asked to host a choir event but only had two weeks to prepare. It was a big task but one that saw over 200 people from our small community in Cwmaman, Aberdare attending. It was an amazing night with a good number of people responding to the gospel! Since that very night we have continued partnering with Rhys and New Hope Baptist Church in missions and have been truly blessed by it ever since. Rhys's passion for Wales and the gospel is inspiring and infectious. He loves Wales and all things Welsh and because of that many towns and communities in Wales have heard the gospel and many lives have been transformed by the power of God. I am glad to know Rhys and to count him as a personal friend. He is a great example of what it means to live for Christ.

Dale Thomas, Pastor - Hope Church, Cwmaman.

I first met Rhys a couple of years ago in Brynmawr whilst he was in Wales with the New Hope gospel choir. Since then we have met every time he comes to Wales. I have great encouragement and enjoyed much prayer time with him and fellow Christians. We had a prayer evening at the Vale resort last year, a very special and inspiring evening. During his last visit I was pleased to have Rhys spend a day at the Scarlets with myself and the team. His positive presence was appreciated by all the players and coaches. He also joined in our bible study at the end of the day. It's been such a blessing to know and receive great teaching from Rhys. A true man of God!

Byron Hayward, Welsh international, record points scorer in top class Welsh rugby, former Coach Wales under 20's, Defense coach for Scarlets, Pro12 champions 2017.

I first met Rhys in the summer of 2003. Here was a man who not only loved God, but loved Wales as well. He recounted the story of his Grandfather playing rugby for Wales. His eyes were burning with pride and passion. That passion has continued to this day. His love and concern for the valleys has, if anything, grown deeper over time. Our partnership in the Gospel has been inspiring as well as humbling. God has used Rhys to help the Church re-connect with its communities through rugby, song and the gospel. I owe Rhys a great deal as he selflessly gives of himself to serve the Lord here in Wales, to help restore our love for God and Welsh Rugby. I count it an honour to know Rhys as my friend, who continues to inspire many through his love, passion and zeal.

Andy Pitt, Pastor Park Baptist Church, Merthyr Tydfil

Rugby and Revival

Guest editors Laura Treneer, Sophie Duffy

Forewords by Garin Jenkins, Emyr Lewis, David Chilcott, Phillip Deuk,
Byron Hayward, Andy Pitt, Dale Thomas, Rev Ian Burley, John Conrad.

Cover design or artwork by Sarah Stenner and Eleanor Stenner

Prepared for publication by Sarah Stenner
Cover photograph by H. A. Chapman

CONTENTS   Page

Chapter One
<u>Teignmouth 1972</u>

My name is Rhys. I was named after Ronnie Rhys Morris, my Grandpa. He spoke a sentence to me in early 1972 that was like electricity to me, and has in large part shaped my destiny.

I was born within sight of the famous Severn bridge the main link road then between England and Wales. The Queen did the official opening in 1966. I was there, aged just 2, and it rained. My Mum kept the picture that I drew of the Queen holding an umbrella.

We lived a couple of miles away in Thornbury. I was born at home, under the care of the surgery that used to belong to the most iconic cricketer of all Dr W.G Grace.

Eventually the family, moved down to Teignmouth in Devon. But my favorite trip was always to Bristol to stay with "Nanny and Grandpa". I felt like I grew up around Bristol rugby. I loved the Memorial Ground. John Pullin was the Bristol and England captain. At the time he was England's most capped player and had recently beaten New Zealand. He was part of the greatest game and "score" in history. I remember the farmer Pullin coming round to Grandpa's house. I was in awe. My Mum always reminds me that she was in the same class as him at Grammar School and they remembered each other.

I got used to Grandpa being "somebody" at the rugby. On match days Nanny, my grandmother, would join a few ladies and make dinner for the players. It took all day. They did the best shepherd's pie. I was allowed to fold the napkins but easily tired of the kitchen chatter. As I think about it, I probably had muddy hands!

Bristol always had thousands come to the home games. On the alternative week to the 1st XV playing, the second team, the "United" drew a more modest crowd but the same quality dinner. Once Teignmouth came all the way to Bristol and played respectably against the United.

We arrived at about 9 a.m. The matches would kick off at 2.30 p.m. and dinner was served at about 5.00 p.m.

Nanny was eventually made one of the few Vice-Presidents in the club's history, having probably served for as many hours as her hilarious friend, the delightfully named Betty Crabb, one of the great servants of the famous club. The ladies were the backbone. Or in rugby terms, the pack. The men showed up much later for the game, the food and the bar. Not necessarily in that order.

On Saturdays, from early morning, during this long wait, I would dive in and out the stands and run up and down the terraces and then onto the field. Two-aside on the huge field was exhausting! I occasionally asked for a match ball from Nobby the groundsman, who always obliged, and I would try to kick over the posts from the half way line. Inevitably I had to reset my sights! At least I remember kicking one over, aged 11, from the old 25 yard line in front of the committee bar.

I would chat to the players who were always kind to this short, skinny boy as they warmed up on the pitch. The magnificent South African cricketer Mike Proctor was often there.

Of course Pullin was the greatest Bristol player, perhaps of all, but Alan Morley became the official record club try-scorer globally of all-time. I remember passing the ball to visiting England international wing Mike Slemen, before a game. I watched as he dropped goals from far out, the ball would sail over the uprights.

Grandpa even took me to the practice matches. He was Chairman of the Selectors in Bristol's greatest ever season 1957-8. He never had to show a ticket on match day. He would walk in to the old stadium, the Memorial Ground, often with a half a dozen family members in tow. Everyone would shout "Come on Bris." During the game I hoped that the ball would be kicked into touch if it would land close to us. I dreamed of catching the ball in front of all those people as we sat on the committee box two seats from the announcer.

One day, during a dull encounter, Grandpa tired to cajole me into saying "Come on Bris" into the old-style announcer's microphone. I was too shy then. In fact I feared speaking in class at school in those days.

One night the great Welsh valleys team Pontypool were the opponents. A huge crowd was gathered for the evening kick off. The famous "Pooler" pack featured Faulkner, Windsor, Price and captain Terry Cobner, were half of the national team pack of 8 forwards.

I can still hear in my mind the visiting fans banging on the hoardings,

"Pool-er, Pool-er".

I remember that it was a game with a lot of blood and have heard of it being talked of a few times since.

We had a problem before the match. A friend of mine, had the keys to the lighting area. Like me, he was there in no official capacity. While we walked the pitch, with it's long grass, my friend (don't worry I was implicated too) had thrown the keys in the air and totally lost sight of them in the dusk light. We didn't even hear them land. We began looking. A rugby field in those days had grass that could cover your shoes. Soon a larger gathering searched for the keys for some time. Nobby was very unhappy, until they were found and therefore all was well. Then the game was played in front of 10,000. It was a well-remembered occasion or battle. I choose to forget about the keys though.

I loved all my family. It was a happier age in some ways. We didn't have cell phones and we used to talk! But everyone knew that Grandpa and I had a soul-connection. At least it was obvious to me. Or maybe it was that we were both just rugby-mad. He did have an older brother die as an infant and his name was Rhys.

My Mum and Dad, brother Peter and sister Sophie had moved to lovely Devon in 1972. It was the end of the golden era of tourism down on the "English Riviera". We used to travel to stay with my grandparents back in Bristol 100 miles away. But Grandpa and Nanny enjoyed travelling to us every month at the weekend when the Bristol 1st XV were not playing at home! They were quite a pair in the car. Nanny preferred to drive. Whenever they got lost, which was quite often, words were a little heated. Grandpa often napped. He loved the evening TV news. He set his evening around it but he would nod off ten minutes in. The family found this an endearing trait and chuckled especially if he snored.

Growing up in England, everyone played football, including me, all day long. Welshman called it soccer like Americans in those days too, because Football was Rugby! We would play before school, at break, lunch and after school. We would play with a proper ball and if it broke we'd play with a tennis ball or even a stone. I scored some marvelous goals with a stone that was so small we could hardly see it. I probably imagined some of those goals.

There was something about seeing my first rugby match on TV that affected me: Wales v England 1972 at Twickenham, London. I knew I had to cheer for Wales but didn't know why. We were in our lounge in Teignmouth.
Wales were in red. They looked great on the colour TV. I wasn't anti-England, after all Pullin was England captain, and I had lived there all my life. But I was pro-Wales. Just in rugby. I still cheered for England at soccer. Wales took another 40 years to be a major force in soccer.

I had heard of Barry John. He was the kicker, a household name, and his two penalties gave Wales a slim lead, 6-3. The match was tight. It seemed to last forever. Wales also had a player called Morris who has become a new friend. Towards the end of the match someone called John Williams, later to be called JPR after his initials, John Peter Rhys, crashed over the line to score the only try of the match. Wales won 12-3. This was the best game I had ever seen! JPR was interviewed on "Grandstand" afterwards with cuts on his forehead and beaming with joy. It happens that this was the first 4-point try ever scored for Wales. After the match Barry John was requisitioned into the TV show *This is Your Life*. That was unprecedented fame for a rugby player

Later that day I heard the life-changing sentence:

"Grandpa played for Wales".

This explained so much, and why Grandpa seemed to be like a magnet at the rugby. He told me the news very modestly. He was the fly half. Most would agree that Wales have had more great fly-halfs than any other nation throughout the rugby's history. The singer Max Boyce wrote a song about the "fly half factory". From the daring Percy Bush in 1905, to the four greats of the 30's; Cliff Morgan, and Carwyn James in the 50's to Barry John and Phil Bennett in the 70's; Jonathan Davies and more recently Neil Jenkins, Stephen Jones, James Hook and Dan Biggar. Wales adores the fly half.

This may seem strange but it helped me understand who I was, and made sense of my name. Even this day, at the time of writing in Margianno's restaurant in Atlanta, the seating host called me "Rice". I always reply "Rhys". There is a lot in a name, and the words we speak to our children, or grandchildren. Be proud of your name.

The second match in '72 was v Scotland. It was glorious. Scotland were always a busy, skillful, marauding team. But Wales scored some glorious tries in the second half. This was when I realised that this Wales team had several all-time greats: JPR, Gerald

Davies, who was up until he retired surely the best winger ever, "Merv the swerve" and Sir Gareth Edwards, who scored one of the finest tries ever seen in this match.

Rugby was rarely on the TV; so I tried to remember everything I could about the games and tried to replay it over and over in my mind. In fact I still remember a lot of things this way.

But 4 or 5 times a year Wales were on our new enormous 28 inch colour TV screen. The build up to each game was unbearable to me. Worse than Christmas. But I was so proud that Grandpa played for Wales, and Wales were the best. They played with such skill. The crowd would sing hymns, it sounded nothing like the comedic or mean-spirited songs from the soccer terraces. It had a reverence to it that no other nation seemed to produce. I tried to remember the tunes. I had no idea what I was singing but in one way I was singing out part of my destiny.

I tried to learnt the anthem. It took me a year just to learn: "Mae Hen Wlad". There was no internet; so I waited for each game to come around and tried to figure it out.

Grandpa also made me a promise. He would give me his cap.

"What's a cap", I asked.
"This is what you get for playing for Wales," he replied.

Up til this point players got one cap and no more. Not until Gareth Edwards played 50 times did anyone get a second cap. Today there is a cap for a 100th game too and I am proud of my dear friend Garin Jenkins for getting a first cap, 50th cap and also three more, each of his three world cups. The World Cup was 15 years from reality in 1972.

Grandpa was true to his word. Sometime in 1973 he came down to Teignmouth with his cap. I have cared for this legacy, although I know that a legacy is more than fabric. Not many more than 1100 have been given out in a 135 year history and no doubt one or two have been lost.

When Grandpa took Sophie my sister and I to St Fagan's Museum, Cardiff, I was fascinated that the pièce de resistance in the Museum were the caps, including one from 1905. The picture of the team that beat New Zealand to become the first ever unofficial world champions, is one of my favourites. Books have been written on that game alone. I can name most of that team having gleaned all I can on that occasion when Wales won.

There was a time when I would get Grandpa's cap out for match days and lay it reverently out to be seen. But I later realized this was a superstition I did not want to entertain nor be bound by.

I remember the first defeat. To New Zealand. Wales were the better side. Glyn Shaw and Dai Morris from the village of Rhigos, made up a quarter of the welsh pack! Glyn told me recently, on a night when I was the speaker at Rhigos, that he made his debut that day. He and Dai were both in attendance that night and are humble men.

Dai founded the rugby club in Rhigos and I love to visit there with stunning views over-looking the Brecon Beacons. Our choir loved the people of the remote but warm village.

Back to the game, JPR took hold of it by the scruff of the neck in tandem with Gerald Davies. JPR showed remarkable power and courage, Gerald had speed and guile. JPR had a try unfairly disallowed.

It was too much to overcome an early 0-10 deficit. Wales missed a final kick to tie the game and lost 16-19. I watched the game with Grandpa in Teignmouth. I can see the game in my imagination still. Or maybe it is just the YouTube reruns!

Twelves months later a team mainly of Welshman beat New Zealand in a spellbinding win for the Barbarians, that many consider to be the finest game ever. Tries were scored by Gareth and JPR. When Gareth scored early on, I leaped into the air. We were now living in Torquay and Grandpa was not with me for that game. Dad was looking after the shop downstairs selling mainly newspapers and cigarettes. But he heard it on the radio. I ran downstairs to say I had seen the greatest try ever, which it was.

The cap was with me upstairs in front of the colour Tele. The Barbarians were almost Wales then anyway.

Grandpa took me to Wales to see Newport play the Barbarians every Easter Tuesday. Before the game we got autographs from the likes of English captain Billy Beaumont. But I was most excited to get the signature of Welsh grand slam winners like Alan Martin, Terry Cobner, and future stars like Brynmor Williams.

I do most remember when Grandpa got the attention of Phil Bennett, the current Welsh captain, a man of similar height to Grandpa. Grandpa told the brilliant Llanelli "scarlet " (they also play in red) that he also was a Welsh international.

"Which position?"

"Fly half"!

Phil Bennett stopped and chatted for a while. I remember thinking that this was special. Several times since I have been near Phil Bennett again and never got to chat and thank him for honouring a fellow fly half. I will one day.

Rugby was always bigger than the super-star of the day. Life is bigger still. An old cap cannot make you happy. Barry John even sold his. But for me it was part of my destiny and the story has more to it.

Chapter Two
<u>Carmarthen 1933</u>

1905 was a glorious year for Welsh Rugby. Although I have a soft spot for 1976, 1988, 2005, and 2013, 1905 was probably the best.

I loved to read of captain Gwyn Nichols and of that 1905 team. Nicholls developed the game as an innovative thinker, and loved to see others score around him like Rhys Gabe, his relative Bert Winfield, and Willie Llewellyn, whose house was spared in the Tonypandy riots because of the affection for his achievements. Then there was delightfully named Little Dickie Owen and Teddy Morgan who scored the vital winning try.

The fly-half is revered to the Welsh. He is expected to be the play-maker, the quarter back if you like, called to set the game on fire. Percy Bush was the first great name to fill this position in 1905. Reputedly this was the year that communal singing made it to Welsh games. Swansea's Billy Trew, a few years later, accomplished much with the expected brilliance of a Welsh half back.

But something greater stirred in Wales. A 26 year old former-miner called Evan Roberts soon became the most famous name, not only in Wales but some believe in the world. His remarkable prayer-life sparked the Welsh revival of 1904-5. Grandpa's cousin Jim Griffiths was leader of the South Wales Miners Union, and the very first Secretary of State for Wales. This is his personal account as a young teenager from his book Pages from Memory.

"In the year in which I started work 1904, came the "Welsh revival". This was not one of those elaborately organized and expensively advertised affairs as we have seen in more recent times. This was a homespun revival inspired by a young coal miner who had entered an Academy to be trained for the non-conformist ministry. Evan Roberts came to one of the chapels in our village and all our family went to hear him. I do not remember a word of what he said, but I can still see him standing up in the pulpit tall, dark hair falling out of his face, and the quiet voice reaching the gallery as if you were singing. Why did it happen? That is a question beyond me. All that I have are the memories of a boy who had just started work, of how everything started to be suddenly different. There were services down the mine, in which the gaffer took part, and our home was turned into a chapel. For a year or two it transformed life in the valleys, but then it faded out leaving a void".

For Jim Griffiths politics took over. Grandpa was very non-political.

This was a revival especially of young men. There are scores of books written of those passionate days.

The Western Mail stopped reporting sports and reported the thousands of spiritual conversions each day throughout the principality. The fame of this spread globally. The congregational singing was spontaneous, went on all night, and may explain how this has been a feature in Cardiff on international day. May it not be forgotten.

Most were turned off by a light-show before the
Wales v England game 2015. Something more melodic
was needed maybe, more spiritual even, more uniquely
Welsh. Within a decade of the revival, many of these
young men affected by the revival went off and died in
the First World War, where 40,000 Welshman perished.
But it's power is known across the world. The 100th
anniversary of first the revival and then the war have
brought the significance of the era to light.

On June 13th 1913 my Grandpa Ronnie Rhys
Morris was born at 8, St David's Avenue Carmarthen.
"Merlin's town", 1913 was a different era. The great and
terrible First World War was not yet imagined. It
changed so much. Grandpa was born a few months
before World War I. Years later his daughter, my mum,
was born a few months before World War II.

Grandpa was a choir boy but where he shone
was sports. Cricket, football, rugby and athletics. Aged
15, Ronnie played for Carmarthen. He was proud to
have represented the Grammar school, and held pride of
place in a photo he gave me of the 500th anniversary of
the school. He is sitting in the centre between two of
Wales most beloved rugby men, Gerald Davies and Ray
Gravelle.

At 17 years old he was picked to play for the
great club Swansea. People thought he might grow a
little taller. Not much more than 5' 3", he would not have
been the shortest in the famous 1905 team, but by the
1930's he was considered short but stocky, not afraid to
tackle, and very, very fast.

At Queen Elizabeth Grammar School he ran 100
yards in 10.1 seconds, winning athletic medals. He had

footballing skills, turning out a few times for Swansea City Thirds. He played Cricket as a young man in Swansea for The Water Rats cricket team at St Helens. I was not able to find out anything about that team but recently stumbled across a book called Swansea RFC, to find out that this was the rugby club cricket team! I have seen a picture of Grandpa being applauded off the field with bat held aloft after scoring I believe 70-odd that day. He told, me that there were 72 steps up to the famous Pavilion or clubhouse. I thought he looked like me and I wanted to do the same thing. I walked those steps with my daughter Megan in the summer of 2015 as we walked around St Helens, then the largest sports ground in Britain, perhaps for the last time, as the ground may not survive in it's present form.

Grandpa became one of the finest club cricketers on the other side of the Severn turning out for Gloucestershire 2nd XI scoring 52 not out. He scored several hundreds for the Optimists in Bristol, at Blaise Castle. His best was 119 not out against Dorking. He once bowled out the great Wally Hammond who was a friend. He was even closer as a friend to England captain Tom Gravenny. I have no doubt that he could have played cricket professionally.

I visited the "Optimists" ground over the River Avon once with him, and everyone recognized him. I was captain of Teignmouth Grammar by then, and I was hoping I could get a game! He won a special cup for the Optimists in 1937, his most amazing year.

But it was always going to be rugby. In his last year at school, Grandpa played fly half for Wales schools against France. I have a postcard picture of him looking so young. He had three favorite tries. The first was in this game when he ran through the entire French team to score for Wales.

Grandpa played fly half for Wales against Scotland for the first time in 1933. In this decade Wales had four legendary fly-halfs.

Harry Bowcott was considered Wales first great British-Lion tourist. He was a key part of Wales first ever win at Twickenham in 1933. He was a key influencer for years afterwards and a great character. At his death in 2004 he was Wales oldest living international.

Cliff Jones was considered the prince of fly-halfs. A brilliant Cambridge student, Jones seemed to play rugby smiling. He had lightning speed and we can catch a rare try of his on Pathe newsreels. He chaired the selectors in the great Welsh teams of the 70's and Grandpa said they were great friends. Jones was often injured and played surprisingly little club rugby for either Cardiff or Cambridge University. I have spoken to older men who believed that Jones was the best of all.

Then Willie Davies, cousin of Hayden Tanner. He only played six times for Wales, and turned pro playing rugby league "up North", meaning that he turned pro, as an all-time great well into the 1950's.

I have been saddened when I read of the passing of these great men in recent years.

The other was Ronnie Morris.

Only 15 rugby union Welshman have been voted into the Welsh Sports Hall of Fame. Remarkably one was

Cliff Jones and one Willie Davies. Bowcott was brilliant too.

It is amazing that Grandpa, this little fellow, got picked for Wales despite 2 of the 15 hall of famers being in his position at his time. But aged only 19, Carmarthen's famous son got the call.

The day he was selected, it seemed that the whole town came round to 8 St David's Avenue and cheered. They went for a run around in the park afterwards. I have imagined the scene so often, I almost think that I was there. What a moment to imagine.

I played golf at Carmarthen in 1989 and asked if anyone remembered Grandpa,

"Oh we were proud of him", replied the club secretary.

In the 1930's there were no team sessions. You showed up to play. These were Amateur days. To practice was to err. There began the tradition of the nation being the unofficial selector of teams. Today's coach, Warren Gatland, loves to give his team a chance to redeem themselves after a defeat, and is adept at avoiding back to back defeats. In the old days huge changes of selection occurred.

For many years I could only imagine what Grandpa was like as a player. The words I heard were "side-step", "drop goal" and "quick". Two Bristol publications use the phrase "astounding pace". We walked over the St Helen's turf once together. I was all questions. He described the pitch as perfect, the best, and "springy". Recently the groundsman told me that it is one of the best draining too.

Another cousin of Grandpa's told me that Morris was not just well-known but famous. I could only imagine. But thanks to my good friend Tim Lawrence, at Brighton Library, I obtained a video of the 1933 game, and one from 1937. Today you can get Pathe clips on-line very reasonably. Most clips last about a minute and a half.

Grandpa often recounted that he was in the first ever televised rugby club match. It was Bristol v Harlequins. I have never been able to find it though.

But I have analysed every available frame of my Grandpa playing for Wales v Scotland 1933. The sound doesn't work. But the headline is "Playing Field becomes Mass Choir". We have to guess when the music was played. Interestingly the entire crowd wear hats, and to watch them take them off is quite a sight, like a field of corn blowing in the wind.

I have the shirt Grandpa wore. It has a large letter F on the back. When playing for Wales schools, he wore the number 6. Today a fly half wears 10, but the position is the same. Some call it stand off, some fly half or outside half. But you can see him wearing that shirt. His stature makes it obvious too.

Scotland were a strong team. A few years previously Eric Liddell ran down the Scottish wing several times as a "Chariot of Fire"!

On one occasion in the 1933 game, we can see Grandpa forced to defend and bravely flings himself on the ball, as we see the Scottish forwards pile over him. I sense a joy in Grandpa's play.

In the pre-match official photograph, he has a big smile, and next to him, like a true Welshman, a leek, the

Welsh national vegetable, is placed next to him on the grass. Just as in the 1905 photographs, the fly half sits to the right and the scrum half to the left. The next time he plays for Wales he will be sitting next to the remarkable Hayden Tanner.

Wales lost the game. Bowcott came back in with a strong midfield with Wilf Wooler, Claude Davey and Viv Jenkins. Wales then beat England for the first ever time in 23 years of trying at Twickenham. Grandpa was pleased for the win and always cheered for Wales. I watched a lot of rugby with him. I once sat between Grandpa and JPR's father, also a doctor I believe. He wore a trilby hat, was full of passion for the match, but was kind to his neighbours who still cheered for Bristol, despite the Welsh team, Bridgend, being the visitors. We saw JPR in the changing room afterwards, along with the centre and kicker Steve Fenwick. JPR was the Rothmans Year Book world player of the year in that year 1976. He signed the book. He was a hero to me. He never lost to England in 11 attempts.

Grandpa would applaud all scores and good play. He just clapped a little louder for Wales, and Bristol.

After the cap, he continued to play for Swansea. His rare speed meaning that as Brinley Matthews said he could "take a pass in any position". Remarkably over four seasons aged 17-21 he was never dropped for a game. The book *The Swansea Story* by Brinley E Matthews and *The All Whites: The Life and Times of Swansea R.F.C.* by David Farmer have quite a bit about Grandpa.

Very few teenagers have ever played for Wales. Most recently Gavin Henson, Tom Prydie and George North have done this with aplomb. Though only North really held his place initially. Keith Jarett, a teenage sensation in 1967 v England, was very influential, but his talents attracted the scouts and he "went North". Grandpa may have been the second youngest player to play for Wales in the first 50 years.

When he moved to Bristol for business at the end of 1934, Wales was in a severe economic depression. His story tells a little of the history of Wales as the nation adapting to tough times. Many had to leave their families behind. He never went down the mine like his famous cousin. But he was like a modern day sportsman as he worked as a sales rep whilst playing rugby and cricket.

Rugby Union was until 1995 an amateur sport as was the Olympics, allegedly. France were banned in the thirties because of violations of the amateur code. Wales were almost banned after fans raised money for the brilliant Arthur Gould to buy a house.

In 1995 after the "Invictus" game, made into the movie starring Matt Daemon, Rugby Union could now be pro.

As hard times came to Wales, many of the best players up until then amateur, took a fee and "went North" to play in the different rugby league 13-man code, turning professional and therefore never being able to play for Wales again. In fact players that did this were not welcome back to their home grounds. It was said that 25% of Welsh internationals left Wales this way. One was Willie Davies. Another from the 30's was a full back called Jack Bassett who one older man told me years ago was better than JPR! The same man preferred Cliff Jones at fly half to Barry John.

Grandpa was offered terms whilst still in Swansea. He refused. I think he loved his sport too much. He was principled but would have not held it against anyone who did.

As the Severn Bridge wasn't built until 1966, I cannot say that he crossed the bridge. But he made it over to the historic city of Bristol, with the marvellous Clifton Suspension Bridge, the Hippodrome where he took my Mum to see Laurel and Hardy live, and the church where Wesley was converted, leading to another great revival in centuries before in the 1740's.

Grandpa loved Bristol. He was happy in his work and in 1937 he got engaged to a feisty English lass called Barbara. She regretted never seeing him pay for Wales.

They had been going out for a short time when he got her tickets for his second international match. She was too shy to go. She was only 19. In later years this was hard to believe but she was young. These were different days.

A few players would get picked for Wales playing for English clubs, but not many. Grandpa made his presence felt quickly in the great club Bristol. Though known for his side-step and swerve, his football skills were vital.

In those days a drop goal was worth 4 points. He had been top points scorer 1932-3 season scoring 62 points at Swansea, including 12 tries. He managed to top-score at Bristol too. He was leaving Swansea as the legendary scrum half Hayden Tanner was arriving, but their paths would cross again, not least the next season when he helped Bristol beat Swansea 3-0. In the 1934-5 season he twice intercepted passes v Swansea, making a try the first time and scoring with the second. It is rare for the same player to intercept twice in a game. I am sure that his speed was a factor.

Grandpa left Swansea a few months too early to face the New Zealand All Blacks. Swansea became the first club side to beat them in 1935. Willie Davies had replaced Grandpa. This was Swansea's finest hour in the first 100 years of their history. Grandpa had apparently linked well with Billy Trew Jnr while at Swansea.

I do love to look at the star-studded Crawshays team picture, April 1937 with Captain Crawshay himself, including Willie Davies and Hayden Tanner. Grandpa stands there in what was an "annus mirabilis" or "marvellous year" for him.

In a recent Bristol program, it is said that he "dropped 28 goals" in 1934-35. Over 100 points in those days. No wonder he was called "Ronnie the drop."

He may have been not only one of Bristol's greatest servants but also players. The history of Bristol RFC 1888-1945 has a featured summary of his life. Both the main histories of both clubs draw attention to his talents. He played 105 times for Bristol. His combination with scrum half Percy Redwood was a great partnership.

His greatest sporting year was 1937. He was picked again, at fly half for Wales v Scotland at St Helen's. The picture shows him stockier, more determined. The Pathe newsreel shows him running inside Wilf Wooler as the tall centre tears away and scores a remarkable try at the end of the ground, where the great cricketer Sir Garfield Sobers of the West Indies would 31 years later hit his world record sixth of six sixes in an over. The ground was a funny shape, as both top class rugby and cricket was played there. It was said that 70,000 could squeeze in the ground, but I heard someone quip that thousands couldn't even see the pitch!

Outside the international arena in England the only official championship was the county championship. Grandpa, like the great Gwyn Nicholls, played for Gloucestershire. This was to be their year and it would not happen again for nearly 40 years.

The Morris-Redwood half-back combination received rave reviews in the London Times archives.

I have a newspaper cutting of the semi-final from the Bristol Evening Post. The interview took place 40 years later. Grandpa was awarded a drop goal in the semi-final v Middlesex. The kick was so high over the posts that it was hard to tell if it was good. But the referee awarded it. (Incredibly in a world cup match in 2011 James Hook did the same thing against South Africa, and the video technology was not used to show that it was actually good! Wales lost by a point in a game they should have won.)

Grandpa accepted the fortunate break and Gloucestershire were in the final at the Memorial Ground Bristol. I have the picture of a packed house and Redwood passing to Grandpa. The ball has come from the line-out, and is half way to Grandpa as he stands perhaps 10 yards away from the scrum half. The pass seems flat, and accurate. Morris seems to be taking the ball at full-pace at a clever angle. He is running straight and you don't know which way he will step or pass. It was close to where we lost the keys!

The Times archive describes how he loved taking a pass at speed, and how he often ran back to cover using his low centre gravity to swoop down on the ball.

His athleticism stands out. He doesn't seem smaller than anybody now. The Times describes their perfection as a unit that day. But in the 1930's the rules made it hard for scores to be many. Often 3-0 would win. My mum was taken by Grandpa to the only England/Wales game that finished 0-0.

Well the final of the national county championship was also 0-0, but there was one score to come. Grandpa was heavily marked and he told me how he took a heavy tackle. He was near the touch-line and threw up. The moment he considered his best in a sporting career, lasting 20 years, was yet to come. I remember him saying modestly,

"Play came back my way, I took the pass, I cut inside and went under the posts".

He had scored the only try, the winning try. It was converted and he had captained Gloucestershire to the English County Championship, the only official rugby championship outside the 5 nations. (Grandpa himself officially proposed the formation of the John Player Cup years later).

He lived for almost 50 years in Bristol, Gloucestershire or both.

The biggest reason for Grandpa playing only twice for Wales despite at least 200 major games for Swansea, Glamorgan, Bristol and Gloucestershire, was not that there were only 19 international matches that he conceivably could have played in that decade, nor Cliff Jones, nor Willie Davies but Adolf Hitler.

Chapter Three
<u>Normandy 1944</u>

1938 was the year "little Ron" was married, and also when he joined the army. He was only 25. He "turned out for Bath a few times in the war" as I recall and then captained Bristol United in the first season after the war. In effect the war ended his career, along with a cartilage operation.

He turned his ankle over many times and in later life struggled with one swollen ankle in particular. I sense that today some key-hole surgery would have had him back playing in a few weeks.

His daughter Mary was born on Feb 3rd 1939, followed by David, Elizabeth and John. Life was changing. The war was worrying. Barbara had much to fear with a young family. Barbara and Mary were evacuated to Carmarthen during the Blitz. David their second child was born there. Grandpa became the PT instructor in the army, and refereed the boxing!

Grandpa went over to France with the "Gloucesters" six days after D-day or D-Day Plus 6. He was in the artillery. He talked about the "percussion fuse", a new sort of guided shell that could take out a plane without directly hitting it. I am told that he had to help "clean out" the destroyed German tanks. I remember him saying that the Canadians were brave fighters and good allies. It is often rare for a man to share a great deal about the war so I wish I knew a little more.

He was at the liberation of Dunkirk and went all the way to Germany. There was a German watch in his collectables, as well as a flag from Dunkirk. But don't tell anyone.

My brother Peter took an interest in Grandpa's war years and encouraged him to send off for his medals and standard issue bar of chocolate. It was quite a thrill when the Ministry of Defence sent the items to Grandpa 30 years later. Peter cherished this part of Grandpa's life and I connected with him over the rugby as may be evident.

The picture of Grandpa with the Bristol team after the war shows a tired looking group of men. If ever there was a just reason for war, this was the one. But they had seen what man should not have to see.

Nanny and Grandpa received a generous gift from the community along with others in the military forces. This helped them buy a house and they lived out their life in the north side of Bristol always, I think, in Gloucestershire. They did live in London for a short while. Their flat was flooded by accident and it was not long after that they were back in Bristol. Grandpa always seemed to be smoking a pipe. It used to fascinate me to see the pipe lit-up; the flame seemed to dance.

Apparently on a trip from London to Bristol he could smell burning. Instead of stopping his car, he opened the window to fan the flames. He discovered, as he arrived home, that his trousers had been singed leaving some embarrassing holes. I inherited Grandpa's limitations on the practical side of household life.

Grandpa I believe was influential as Chairman of Selectors for Bristol, when fly half John Blake encouraged a fast flowing running rugby. Grandpa was proud of a try that Bristol scored in his time as a player that was worth describing. This was his third favourite.

He took a mark or fair catch just in front of his own posts. In those days the defender stood at the mark and the kicker retreated. He was almost on the dead ball line. He kicked, and the ball hit his own cross bar. The ball came back into his hands. He started running and a sweeping passing movement involving half the team, led to a try 105 yards later.

Grandpa formed his own business. He seems to have had the rare qualities of leadership, a winsome business manner and fiscal wisdom. He was always well dressed. In fact writing brings back images long forgotten. I can see again that big winter coat, hat and driving gloves, used always in his new Ford Cortina. His plain black smart shoes made a loud sound on the ground.

He always returned home and gave Nanny a big kiss. We loved visiting his work place. Morris, Oakley and Biggar advertised in the Bristol rugby programme and did so well that in the warehouse the rolls of carpet, and samples of floor coverings seemed an exciting place for my siblings, cousins and myself to run around. My sister Sophie recalls how Grandpa could recognise just about any type of wood like parquet or oak. Carpets eventually became the leading fashion. Perhaps today the business would be thriving again as fashion or even as practicality has returned full circle.

The recession of 1982 hit very hard just when Grandpa had semi-retired and was ill.

They settled in a beloved family home in the 70's called the Paddocks in Easter Compton. I stayed for at least five full summers with my sister Sophie, who is now an author, whilst my parents ran a busy summer business in Torquay and brother worked on the boats in Teignmouth from where today he runs a marine engineering company. Peter kept a keen interest in my father being in the Royal Navy but he had a summer in Bristol with us too.

I played cricket all day and sometimes tore up Grandpa's lawn with my friend Chris who is today Dr Chris Till, but Grandpa understood. One summer Chris and I watched every ball of a cricket Test Match on TV, all 5 days for 6 hours and played cricket in between each session!

Summers were always sunny. We drank gallons of lemon squash. Nanny took us to the zoo, Blaise Castle and the remarkable S.S. Great Britain. We got to these places in her little brown van. We sat in the back with no seat belt or seat, sliding around on a musty foam mattress. As we turned each corner was it great fun and we weren't injured too much! Peter had a whole summer with us and though he enjoyed it, he found his calling early in life: to work by the sea.

I was often happiest with a ball in hand. Cricket was my best sport. This in time became golf. My Dad introduced me to the game during this era. I will never forget being given my first go on a real course, Dawlish Warren, a real links course, so close to the sea that once two entire holes were swept away. I stood on the old 9th tee. It was a long par 4 of well over 430 yards into a a stern wind. I had a cut down 8 iron and I was about nine years old. Before I swing the club I looked in and asked Dad,

"What par is it?"
"Never you mind" he said.

Our family still loves to play all sports in the garden. My girls can all hit the ball with a straight bat, but our youngest Sarah, having lived most of her life in the USA "slogs" the ball effectively as if it were baseball.

My "Field of Dreams" moment would definitely include playing cricket in the garden with Dad or Grandpa or Uncle John.

One summer Elvis died. We watched the news that August 16th 1977 exactly 18 years before the day Louise and I would be married. We didn't plan it that way.

Nanny kept in touch with Betty Crabb who gave me a British Lions badge that once belonged to the Irish legend Mike Gibson, in my view the best Irish Rugby player of all. But don't tell Brian O'Driscoll. We visited her relatives scattered around Bristol. I recently bumped into some of them at a funeral.

Grandpa would often take us on his sales calls and spend the rest of the day with us. We went to places like the Forest of Dean and Cheltenham. We went down to Carmarthen each year to see his sisters Ethel, Doreen and Gwen. His younger brother Granville died when I was small. He had been shot in the leg in the war and my mum was always fascinated by the hole in his leg. It was a seven hour round trip in those days. This was the home where Grandpa lived when he was first picked to play for Wales. We used to pop down to the cycle track. The sloping sides were amazing. I never saw anyone riding on it though. Our great aunts talked so fast with their west Wales accent. They would ask Grandpa if the remembered so and so and then they'd say, "he's dead" most seriously.

Grandpa was with us when the Queen visited Bristol as part of her Silver Jubilee celebrations in the summer of 1977. There was also a medieval festival with jousting. We loved it. We even had a toffee apple. The Queen arrived on time, in a Land Rover. Grandpa insisted that the Queen waved especially for Sophie when they drove by only 15 feet away. Sophie knows she did. It was the second time I had seen the Queen, and the possibly the last.

As I got older Grandpa occasionally dropped me at a Gloucestershire cricket match. Nanny packed me a sandwich, a sunhat which I rarely wore, and 50p. Grandpa met me under the massive scoreboard with about an hours play to go. The most memorable day was when the awesome West Indies came to play. Wayne Daniel was the form bowler, fast and dangerous. They were unbeatable. But that day Alastair Hignell the Bristol Rugby full back, and later BBC commentator, scored a century. He got his hundred hitting a six over midwicket and the crowd went wild. I went wild and I am not sure I have ever felt so proud of a local lad achieving so much against a world class outfit.

Cricket was such a contrast. Rugby is played half the season in cold and wet with a muddy pitch. As a junior rugby player it took endurance for a skinny kid to stay warm. The knocks seem to hurt so much more when cold. Then the warmth of summer. Though hitting a ball incorrectly on a brisk spring day or stopping a hard shot could cause the hands to wince.

One favourite memory is training at "The Paddocks" with my uncle. Grandpa's youngest son John was scrum half at the time, with perhaps the best team in England, Rosslyn Park. But like me, his heart is for Wales. I had seen him help Saracens thrash Torquay the year before at the Recreation Ground where I played cricket.

He now played behind Number 8 Andy Ripley one of rugby's legends and characters. Uncle "JVH" had a long spin pass. So he stood 15 yards away and threw it to me. I was 11. Grandpa was teaching me to run onto the pass and hit it at pace. Looking back on it, that was very special. But it felt it at the time too. When I returned to rugby aged 26 at Teignmouth, I said I was a fly half, though I had payed most of my junior rugby at scrum half.

It was a novelty to have a Baptist Minister in the team and the language of the team greatly improved without me saying a word about anything. But a concussion and a popped rib from a late tackle said that I was still perhaps not bulky enough, and with a baby on the way Louise preferred I watch the games. She has been supportive of my rugby passion and seen a few big games with me.

Garin Jenkins affirms my rugby prowess by saying that I have watched a lot of rugby! Today concussion has detailed protocols. In those days they put me at full-back.

Those summers in the 70's were long and hot. I often would go upstairs and gaze out the window and look at the Severn Bridge. The sunsets in this part of the world were considered some of the finest on the planet. It was a stunning sight. Meanwhile two miles away Concorde was being developed. One day it flew over The Paddocks three times, within half an hour, barely 300 feet over the house. Maybe a touch more. Another day I saw Concorde fly over the bridge. This would be a parable of my life. A bridge first between England and Wales and later to the USA with the two connecting. I would look at this view endlessly. A cap and a bridge and an airplane.

Grandpa loved games being played on his lawns. Nanny planted exotic plants usually cuttings from other exotic gardens! Blaise Castle must have the biggest lawn in the world. The wide expanse of grass must have stretched half a mile or so it seemed. They used to live right next to it.

My Grandmother took us over the Clifton Suspension Bridge and ended up on her knees due to the incredible height. I have never been the same with heights. She often told the story of a unhappy lady who threw herself off the bridge, something to do with love gone wrong. Her Victorian skirts acted as a parachute and she was rescued having landed softly and wedged into the mud of the River Avon. The lady lived to have a long and happy life.

One theory of Grandpa choosing the Paddocks as a location was that he could get the TV signal for both BBC and ITV for England AND Wales. When the English "Rugby Special" finished, he could watch the

Welsh equivalent of "Scrum Five". He loved the insight of Carwyn James the fly half turned coach who beat New Zealand with three different teams. A double dose of rugby.

One of my favourite stories was on Christmas Eve. Most of the family had popped out to "see the vicar" a euphemism for gone to the pub. Peter had managed to blag his way out of the house whilst I was left behind. So it was me, Sophie, Grandpa and Nanny. With the excitement of the night unbearable for the children, we were in high spirits. So when Nanny said it was bed-time, I hid behind a thin mattress that was out to accommodate a family member. I heard Nanny get worried:

"Rhys...Rhys...Rhys."
Her pitch got higher.
She got more frantic.

Suddenly, I realised that I could be in big trouble. So I began to crawl out, tempting though it was to stay.

Grandpa saw me crawling out. I looked at his eyes. He looked at me. We paused. Then he whispered "get back in" and proceeded to keep calling my name saying, "I have no idea where he is!"

To be fair to Nanny, she was a good sport over it.

On another occasion Nanny took us to the joke shop.

That night, we set a tiny air pump under Grandpa's place-mat that could wobble his soup. We squeezed the air, but it was so imperceptible that Grandpa didn't notice. I think that Nanny had to explain the cunning plan in the kitchen between courses and Grandpa played along. He could be seen the rest of the evening deliberately walking around in his favourite slippers with a squeaking noise that we had also set-up. All Grandpas have to be ready to be at the end of a joke.

Grandpa had to watch the news every night. So at 9 o'clock we had to be still. But he would always fall asleep after ten minutes. He loved the news.

The centre of gravity seemed to shift from Easter Compton, to Bristol back to Teignmouth, Devon as my Dad had a couple of set backs.

We began a guest house in the Fawlty Towers comedy show era, starring John Cleese, only eight miles from the original. I was the "head-waiter" and named myself Manuel. Nanny and Grandpa often came to stay. He watched me play mini rugby for Teignmouth a few times, though he missed my first try. I played scrum half, which meant I could spin pass like, I thought, Gareth Edwards, though the dive-pass meant less late-tackles. My first try was scored in a blizzard. They couldn't see me. It reminds me of the try Rhys Gabe scored. As Wikipedia has recorded, and I have read this in various accounts,

"His most remarkable try was probably one scored against England at Bristol in 1908. The match was played in thick fog, and Gabe and his team mate Percy Bush found a loose ball outside England's 25. Gabe won the tussle for the ball and set off in the direction of the line, while Bush ran off in the opposite direction to confuse the opposition. Eventually the referee and the other players arrived at the line to find Gabe waiting with the ball."

In 1978 my Father went missing. Nanny and Grandpa came straight down. They had a look of great concern for their eldest daughter and grandchildren. The next morning we saw a police light over the fence at the end of the garden. This was ominous. The kind police officer arrived with our elderly neighbor Peggy married to Major Carter, a man of warmth like the Major on Fawlty Towers.

Sophie and I were hurried upstairs. The wait was unbearable. Peter was on a deep sea fishing trawler off the Cornish Coast. We came downstairs without being asked. My Mum had to tell us, "I am afraid that Daddy is dead".

These were different days, we Brits didn't always know how to talk about things. I put this down less to a somewhat harsh image of the influence of Victorian Britain and more to the unprecedented wave of grief that followed the death of 900,000 young men form 1914-18 followed up by many more thousands who died in what we still call The War, or World War Two.

It became apparent that Dad had taken his life. He had been injured on board ship while serving as a midshipman years before in the Royal Navy. Dad trained at Dartmouth Naval College and loved ships. He served on HMS Tiger and HMS Ark Royal. His chosen career was over. The back injury only really got worse. He was in pain a lot of the time. He had two six month spells with his back in a full plaster cast. One day, I remember that he walked around Dawlish Warren Golf Club watching me play for 9 holes while "bound" this way. He borrowed my tiny 8 iron, at the end of the round, and chipped the ball from 60 yards to six inches from the pin. I was amazed. There were other life-struggles of course.

I gave a talk in our Church in 2014 that is still on our New Hope web-site, *"To those left behind"*. We survivors of events like this don't often talk about ourselves or have awareness campaigns, but there are more of us than we know. I have seen that most of the "left behind" have compassion and become somewhat expert in the factors that assailed our loved ones.

But all know that suicide is very painful to those left behind and we take a long time to figure it all out. Suicide does not end pain, it just passes it on to others. Please never give up hope. We must determine not to be defined by our past sorrows.

I know that Dad loved us. I think he persuaded himself that we were better off without him. That is never true. But that is a state of mind that some sadly get locked in. I do know that he had a great sense of humour, a fine intellect and loved us all. He played golf to a high standard. Though I have made it at one time not too long ago to scratch with the USGA, I am sure that with modern technology his 3 handicap in the UK was much better than scratch in the USA today.

He missed the outlet of being able to play as his body weakened. But 45 is too young to die.

I know my Dad would have loved to have seen some of my great golf experiences including playing Augusta. Louise and I stayed in the Butler Cabin where the green jacket is presented, and where Eisenhower used to stay. That day in 2009, we were one of only two foursomes all day. Golf heaven. Dad played St Andrews several times, something I have never done. It was a pleasure meeting Arnold Palmer a few times also as well as playing a round with Justin Rose and Tom Kite. But I am happy playing with anybody as long as they don't concede their own putts from 6 feet!

Grandpa and Dad got on well. I remember Dad really enjoyed watching rugby with Grandpa. Dad cheered for England with good humour and in the 70's he needed it. But he was always pleased for me when Wales won. Now he was gone. I remember thinking immediately that I would never see him again.

The next few days Grandpa said things to me that were designed to strengthen me,

"You must be a brave boy".

My Grandpa who played for Wales, and who played his part in defeating Hitler, was calling on me to show courage.

The shy boy born near "the bridge" found a strength beyond himself. One month before my Dad died something happened. Like most Brits at the time I thought I was a Christian because I was British! We were like most families in England, "christened in Church of England" but not attending Church, except for school carol services, which remain enduringly popular. Being Christian meant moral and kind. But there was less about Christ. My Mum did read me bible stories from a bible picture book that I had loved as a child. I was always fascinated with why Jesus died on the cross. I remember asking at school, "why did he die"?

No-one could really answer that one.

Then at school, when I was 11 at Greylands School, Paignton, I won a class prize, which was a Bible. I read slowly through the Old Testament and developed a sense of the holiness of God without knowing the phrase.

We moved from Teignmouth to the much larger town of Torquay. We saw Torquay United take the lead against Tottenham Hotspur with 24,000 packed in. But Spurs replied with 4. World Cup Winner Martin Peters played, as did the great "goalie" Pat Jennings. I can still remember nearly all the Spurs team. But none from Torquay.

Sophie and I went to a small school that did have a strong sense of the Bible during this time.

We moved back to Teignmouth from Torquay. My brother and I gained entrance to the Grammar School

One day my future best man Al told me something that defined me even more than "Grandpa played for Wales". Al was a highly intelligent, witty, creative, and badly behaved boy. He could be kind. Except to authority!

At the time Pink Floyd's "Brick in the Wall" sounded the anti-authority note. Then came punk rock.

This seemed to give Al a philosophy to justify the rebellion. Or perhaps he was just less afraid than the rest of us for getting into trouble. But a change had come over him. His temper became kindness. He went from a literal hooligan to peacemaker. He was told that his new faith was a "flash in the pan",but he is as strong as ever in the belief that has been his guide to now most of his life.

On November 28th, 1978, one month before Dad died he explained that God was holy and I was not. As I had often asked why Jesus died in my past, this statement made sense. I believed that Jesus had died for a reason. Al explained that it was to be the <u>bridge</u> between me and God. I am sinful, heaven is perfect and Jesus alone could mediate the problem. Nothing else can. (See Acts 4:12).

This made sense. He showed me chapter and verse. And I knew it was true. This was for real. I left school that day, after praying a simple "sinners prayer" with Al, knowing that this was it. It is. I now know the One it is all about. This was the most important day of my life for it has set my trajectory more than receiving a Welsh cap. I hope that this is obvious from this point on.

But I need to tell you how that my Grandpa playing for Wales remains a cherished part of the story. What we have been through is never wasted, and our passions can be directed for greater things.

1978 was not a bad year for a Welsh rugby fan to realise that there was more to life! Wales won the Grand Slam and didn't do this again for 27 years. There was something of the end of the era feeling and so it was. The third golden era of Welsh rugby ended somewhere between 1978 or 1979. Though Wales thrashed England, and won the triple crown in 79, it was not quite the same. Sir Gareth retired and the mercurial Phil Bennett, who had replaced Barry John, accomplished perhaps even more in his career scoring two tries in his last Grand slam-winning game as captain. Sir Gareth played in every Wales game from 1966-78 and was matchless as the greatest player of all. Gerald Davies, the most delightful of men retired after that summer too.

I cared greatly that we won the game against a very strong France to seal the 1978 triumph. Wales won well. But some looked a little tired. I had a strange thought, "I can die happy". It was a foolish thought.

That November I learned that eternal things matter most, not rugby. Death shattered our home. And just 30 days before Dad died I found out that I had a Heavenly Father. This helped me completely. Though grief is always a reality, we can have an anchor in the storm.

Grandpa's words still carry weight to me. They were the same words that King David said to Solomon. "Show yourself a man".

But I learned that manliness is not in rugby or drink or war or anything else. Grandpa and Nanny supported my baptism in March 1979.

After I had prayed the prayer of commitment, Al took me to church with a few friends. We discovered that a new minister was in town at Teignmouth Baptist church, a place that will become a centre of gravity for me for the next 14 years.

The church was declining and down to about 60 members. The famous man of faith George Muller had pastored the Ebenezer Baptist church in Teignmouth. Then there was no Baptist church in the town until 1887. Muller went off to found the Bristol orphanage. But the church in 1978 was small with about 40 in attendance.

Rev Ian Burley arrived in his mid 30's and was told that he would be the last minister that the church had. He was told that there was six months money left. Faith was low.

Al and I met with Ian and a few other young people in the vestry. Within 6 months the church was growing fast. Soon there would be 30 or 40 of us in the young fellowship. Our faith was on fire and the local Grammar School allowed a punk rocker and his skinny friend, whose Grandpa played for Wales, to lead the school assemblies.

The church grew. In fact it was like an explosion of joy, and the people fell in love with Ian and his wife Barbara.

He was the best visiting pastor I have met. He worked incredibly hard. But not only did he do the small things but he had a big vision and we were encouraged to be a part of it. As the church grew, soon the 220 seater chapel was too small. We had to have summer services in the local Theatre that seated 300 and then the Riviera Cinema seating 400. It was national news. We were officially the fastest growing Baptist Church out of 2000 churches then in the UK. This happened in less than two years. The summer of 1983 the church featured on the BBC radio service. It included a Punch and Judy show!

Ian preached winsomely but with the same clear gospel message that had changed me and Al. The singing was electrifying and to be honest we had few special musical gifts. It was the people that sang, like only the Welsh can!
We could happily sing for hours.

The list of activities that followed was incredible:

Open Air services, beach missions, coffee bars, a counselling centre, prayer meetings, partnership missions, a drama group, carnival outreach, We had 1000 on the green space called "The Den" long before the huge band Muse played to their home town! We brought drums into church. And guitars.

Ian was brilliant with Al and myself and a growing church. He encouraged us to use our gifts. I grew in courage. We were well taught. Ton Daniel was our youth leader and a mentor and hero. He rebuked us when we got full of ourselves. We had fun and yet took it seriously.

And I was baptized by immersion. To many in the U.K. this was a strange thing. I gave a simple, testimony in front of about 200 folks that night. Grandpa was there.

"Jesus is everything to me." I said.

They say that the 1904-5 Welsh revival sparked to life when young Florrie Evans declared to sniggering friends, "I love the Lord Jesus with all my heart".

I am grateful for Grandpa being there that night. And he came to the Christmas candlelight service in Teignmouth the next year. He got Candle-wax all over his tweed jacket but took it with good grace. It was a packed Church. Pastor Ian asked me to read out something. I had sung a contemporary song in the atmospheric service, and then I was asked to read out a note, that the Church was sending me on a trip to Dallas, Texas, where I would be the guitarist and singer on our first partnership mission. It was a complete surprise. It was 1980 and we actually did visit South Fork ranch, during the season that JR was shot on the huge TV series *Dallas*.

My life was changing. I felt a call for this to be my life-mission. I still cheered for Wales and loved it when Nanny and Grandpa came to stay. But there is more to life than sports. I wept every time they went home. I was never sure why. I didn't realize how ill he was perhaps.

I think that this was the final lesson my Grandpa taught me. He was dying of cancer still only in his 60's. Today it is possible that it would have been caught earlier and he could have outlived that illness. Most do today.

With my Morris 1300, I drove to Bristol, June 1982 and stayed for a week. The old summers had gone. This was a colder season. I wonder if my tears each time I said goodbye were grief ahead of time, to show them how much I cared. Grandpa praised me for my tea-making ability. Like him I was not good with DIY; so we need encouragement. My wife Louise also praises me for my tea-making skills!

I talked to him about rugby. He still had his Bristol RFC Life Members annual pass. He wrote a W or L next to the fixture after it had been played. The grip on his pen was weaker. The writing less pronounced.

I remember that one of his party pieces was to catch a fly off a wall with his bare hands. I am sure it was genuine and not that he had caught a fly earlier! I have tried a hundred items and failed each time. Fast twitch. Grandpa was less and less about sport and more and more about family. He wanted to talk about other things. Grandpa's final words to me were "work hard and do well". I think he would have been pleased with us sticking at the life we are called too.

I was called to the ministry. I saw a video in the Teignmouth Baptist church hall of Billy Graham preaching. He preached to more than a billion souls and has been called America's pastor. He may have been a factor in the ending of the Cold War. He is one of the greats. He preached to 24,000 a night in Bristol in 1984. He only preached once in Wales to great effect to a thousand souls, I believe in Pontypridd.

I had no illusion of grandeur but I knew that this was my message. I will share how the churches I have pastored have taken the gospel to we estimate well over 120,000 listeners in Wales, many receiving the message gladly. I was amazed the day I was invited to meet Dr Graham in 2009, in his home and he was keen to hear of the work in Wales.

So I set off to London Bible College now the London School of Theology for three years, encouraged by my pastor Ian. It was September 1982. LST was in Northwood, London. The TV sit-com, *The Good Life*, was filmed around Kewferry Road. Every visitor that came to see us walked there a few hundred yards around the corner.

I had very little money and the Morris 1300 didn't make it for long, so I rode the train and carried my guitar through the underground to Northwood, Middlesex the place where the Falklands campaign was being led at the time.

Grandpa had told me to do what I was called to do with all my might and to work hard. I got a "2:1" Theological Degree which was considered good. I learned much from my mentor and fellow Teignmouthian Dr Derek Tidball who once kindly dedicated a book to me. I also really valued RT France who wrote some excellent commentaries. Principal Michael Griffiths was kind to me, and would give me a lift in his Rover when travelling with his family to Devon. He would hear me preach at Teignmouth a few times. This was very kind of him. Leaders are servants.

In the summers I worked in a bakery. It was hot work.

Grandpa and Nanny continued to visit us more frequently. They argued there and back in the car but were fine whenever they reached their destination!

Though Nanny missed seeing Grandpa playing for Wales, they watched an international match in 1981, Wales v England close encounter in Cardiff. Grandpa cheered for Wales and Nanny for England. It may have been Grandpa's last trip over the bridge. Grandpa didn't mind Nanny cheering for England because by then she was caring for him as he faced cancer. And of course Wales won. Nanny still watched Bristol play regularly 70 years after they first met.

I came home one day from my shift at the bakery one summer, and mum was in the garden. She told me that Grandpa had cancer. She shed a tear.

He struggled. I went with him once to hospital where he had radiation treatment. He never complained. I do remember him being in some pain.

One weekend in Teignmouth perhaps his last in Devon, his back was in great pain. He could not get comfortable. And his vision was blurring.

Hospice Care in the U.K. is a wonderful ministry. Grandpa benefitted from it. Of course my Grandmother cared for him, watched him die and then grieved.

It was snowing outside in London, February 1983 when I received the sad news that Grandpa had died aged only 69. My room-mates Andy Hickford and Neil Hudson understood how much this mattered to me, and they were very sympathetic that day. So was Derek. He came to see me immediately. Louise didn't really know me yet. We only knew of each other.

I went to the funeral with Uncle Dick, catching the train from Paddington Station to Bristol. I would have liked to have visited Grandpa more that season, but I didn't actually have any money for the ride. Dick was married to Grandpa's daughter Liz. Grandpa had ten grandchildren who he loved in equal measure. He never liked anyone not getting along. He was a unifier.

Eloise was the firstborn of Liz and Dick. She played rugby. She is tall and strong, her athletic frame more like her father who played flanker for Saracens and for years was captain of Stourbridge.

Eloise, today a Triathlete, was incredible at rugby. In one half she scored six tries for her team as a junior. She was the only girl on either side. This was deemed as unfair to be so dominant, she was too good, so they swapped her to the other team. She scored 7 for the opposition that half! She was like Jonah Lomu. We have enjoyed Eloise staying with us in America. But we kept the rugby on the front lawn to just passing!

We read notice of his death in the Daily Telegraph in the train-carriage. It said "Ronnie Morris dies". There was a picture in another daily paper. There was brief reference to his two caps in 1933 and 1937.

The funeral service was well done. The vicar mentioned that his second cap was 1935. I nearly corrected him. But resisted!

The undertaker was Bristol legend and England international Austin Shepherd, also a 1983 cup winner, a delightful man. He did the same for Nanny almost 30 years later. Death has a sting. I wept that day again. My identity was no longer in Grandpa playing for Wales. Nor should we find our identity in a cap or heirloom, not even in a loved one, even though it still is a wonderful part of the story.

The summer of 1983 I shadowed Ian as a pastoral assistant. I visited scores of homes with Ian and did some on my own. I leafleted every hotel in the area for our summer services. After seminary I did the same again when I sold showers for a couple of years! I learned so much from Ian. At times he didn't get enough holiday. Without a father, it is easy for me to idealise a mentor.

I was soon to find a wife or maybe she found me.

Chapter Four
<u>Twickenham 1983</u>

I met Louise this year. She took me home from a concert where I was the support singer. Her Warburg car was about the equal of my Morris 1300. We talked and talked. It was like meeting a long lost friend. And she was very pretty. And half Dutch. Very cool.

We were both in single parent families. We went out and our dates were often spent walking around central London, looking at shop windows because we spent all we had on the tube ticket to get there. We must have walked miles each time always around Leicester Square. We walked past Harrods days after the IRA bomb devastated Knightsbridge. Louise loved to pop into *Liberty, Laura Ashley* and *Top Shop.*

We played tennis together and found that we had a lot in common. I coaxed her gently to watch the game on TV as Adrian Hadley scored the winner for Wales at Twickenham in 1984 after a fine break by Bleddyn Bowen. We attended the Laing Lecture together, the only time of the year all students were expected to dress and be sombre. Somehow we got the giggles despite desperately trying not to.

We got engaged, in a field in Hatfield, a small town, where they were pioneering the first heart transplants. I am not sure that we could find it today. In those days you didn't have to capture it for posterity on video. It was simple but real. I had saved up the money for a ring by cycling round some very posh houses in Northwood offering to clean cars. One morning I made

£35 which was a small fortune to me. Soon I saved up enough to go into London, and pick out a small solitaire diamond ring. I had a good idea of what she wanted. I bought it on Bond Street which sounds very posh. I showed the ring to Derek before I proposed to check it was OK. He was a supportive leader always to us.

We married in August 1985 at Leigh Road Baptist, Leigh-on-Sea. Pastor Ian preached, Louise's pastor Geoffrey Fewkes, a Welshman, did the vows and Derek prayed for us.

By then both cars had died and sadly many in our family were going through relational challenges. We had a honeymoon in the delightful Isle of Guernsey where Louise's father still lived though he died a few years later. Louise lost her engagement ring on the beach as we played frisbee on our second day. We tried finding it with a borrowed metal detector from an ex-con called Malchi. We never found the ring on the beach as the tide rushed in.

Guernsey has an unusual number of putting courses. I think we played every one of them and Louise nearly won once. Louise graciously watched a thrilling end to the Ashes series with me too. What a woman!

Somehow after the honeymoon, I made it back to Bond Street and they replaced the ring kindly.

But back to Northwood, 1983. My Uncle John invited me to watch Bristol play in the John Player Cup Final at Twickenham between Bristol and Leicester, just weeks after Grandpa died. Bristol had outshone local rivals Bath almost up till this point. But the tables were turning. As it happens this was the last top level achievement for Bristol apart from being in major promotion battles.

Bristol went down 0-12 rapidly and it looked like a painful afternoon with the larger Leicester crowd totally convinced. But Bristol fly half Stuart Barnes kicked a long-range penalty and then kicked ahead for a Bristol try. It was like a memory was awakened and Bristol were well-led by captain Mike Rafter, who I remember chatting to Grandpa often. Bristol won. It was one of the greatest moments in their history. Uncle John got quite emotional and he just said
"He's smiling up there!"

Louise often says that she is an Essex girl. No-one knows what that is in the USA. We moved back to Teignmouth in 1985. I worked in sales for a couple of years which I really enjoyed. It was a good earthing of theological study. I didn't realise then that this was more or less the career that Dad and Grandpa had too. We immediately plugged back into my home church.

I became assistant pastor at the church in 1987. We loved Teignmouth Baptist Church.

I also played a bit of rugby and enjoyed watching the 1988 Triple Crown for Wales on TV. But life was in Devon. Mum had remarried Ralph who encouraged me to play golf again. Then the senior pastor Jeff left and so I was "holding the baby" on my own. I was the sole pastor for 20 months. We had a full church and saw some wonderful growth.

My first pastor Ian Burley had gone to Wales and I went to stay with him one weekend. He talked to me about spiritual renewal and took me on a trip of the valleys especially Ogmore Vale, where the community had declined due to the closing of the mines. Everything was depressed. Most churches had lost vision or even hope.

We went to meet Mrs Charles, a friendly lady, who was in charge of her church. It was a massive building, a 900 -seater. This classic Welsh nonconformist chapel is like so many which have closed. Sadly the interior of the chapel was covered by an inch of dust. Windows were broken. She remembered it being full, with much joy. It was the centre of the community. This was the world's Bible Belt at the time. But now six ladies met downstairs with a one bulb light, and a small electric fire. This was 1988, and I assume that it all closed down. Something stirred deep within me. Ian lit a fire in me. I wanted to help Wales. Up to this point Wales to me was Carmarthen, Cardiff, where Grandpa took me to see Cardiff defeat Australia in 1978, and Newport. Not the Valleys. In fact people often suggested we were wasting our time going there.

In 1990 we took a choir to give three performances to Welsh Baptist Churches. But that was all.

I had become a fully-fledged Baptist Minister after being interviewed for three days. The interviews were coincidentally in Cardiff for the annual Residential Selection Conference. One of the interviewers, John Davies, a key figure in industry, insisted on walking me around the old Arms Park stadium on the first evening there. He didn't know the significance of all this.

Many assumed that we would eventually move to Wales. Everyone did. But we did not. Despite at least

70 trips there since, we moved next to Brighton and Hove, 50 miles due South of London, by the sea.

We named our first daughter Megan. She is as passionate for Wales as I am. She was not yet walking when we arrived in Hove. We began a new ministry in a fine church.

Not much happened about Wales. But I had ventured to rugby matches a few times. More internationals were being played; so for a minor game we could get tickets.

My first venture did not go well. 1988 Wales lost to Rumania and Jonathan Davies a fly-half of the old brilliant mould went north immediately afterwards. The event seemed to create decline.

But in 1989 I wore Grandpa's shirt to a game. What was I thinking? The same shirt is now 82 years old. Its thickness is in contrast to today's fibres. It has lasted well. They don't make 'em like they used to.

Someone spotted me at an event at St David's Hall before the game. Keith Jarret was speaking. It was Wales v England. Wales were in free-fall having lost every game that season, and England were on the rise, and undefeated. England were huge favorites. Some said it would be thirty points. In no time I was being interviewed on BBC Radio Wales, I think it was Roy Hennessy. I said that Wales would win. I knew they would. I was the only one. Later in the game England seemed panicky and the Welsh forwards led by Phil Davies seemed to draw on a collective rugby memory, as scrum half Robert Jones and fly half Paul Turner played with skill and control, as I imagine did Percy Redwood and Ronnie Morris. It poured with rain and I experienced the delights of the East Terrace at Cardiff Arms Park 17 years after I first saw JPR score that try on TV.

Wales won and I think if the game had gone on all day England would not have scored a try. Some disputed Mike Hall's try, as to whether the ball was grounded. But it happened a few yards in front of me. I had the perfect view. It was good. End of argument. The TV replays didn't have enough frames in those days to tell. But I must tell Mike one day that there is no doubt. I ran on the pitch afterwards with everyone else in the pouring rain. You used to be able to do that in those days, just as one could once also go right up to the rocks of Stonehenge and to the front door of Downing Street.

Up to this point I would say "my Grandfather played for Wales", just a few times. While at Teignmouth Baptist in that time-period, I referred to it in a sermon. This was a rare mention. After the service a strong West Country voice said, " I played against your Grandfather".

I soon got to be friends with Bill Hook. Bill played full back for England in the 50's. In fact I have since seen the famous try on video that Ken Jones scored at Twickenham in 1952 with Bill chasing him in vain. Bill told me that Cliff Morgan and Ken Jones ended his England career!

This was a great discovery. Bill would often attend our church and told how he knew Grandpa also with the Gloucestershire connection. Bill played for Gloucestershire. In 1998 he gave Louise and tickets for Wales v England. We lost 8 tries to 4 after leading 2-0!

The actual points number is too hard to mention. I was chuffed to get a smile from the Welsh war-hero Sir Tasker Watkins and didn't release he was sitting next to Prince Edward. That day reminds me of my friend Bill and that saying that "Grandpa played for Wales" brought amazing results! We sat among men who knew Grandpa.

Those who have loved ones are always thankful when others remember them.

Chapter Five
<u>Troederhiw 1994</u>

"His Grandpa played for Wales or something", he said to Dave Chilcott who was the post master of Troederhiw, South Wales. Dave was also the lay pastor of the Tabernacle Church. I had asked Phillip Deuk, my dear friend, to see if we could do anything for Wales. Phillip had just joined the staff at Holland Road, Hove. When I say the staff, it was just me, Phillip and part-time secretary Olwyn in those days. Phillip somehow had got in touch with Dave and his wife Jean.

By October 1994 we did our first proper mission to the Welsh valleys. The plan was to go, serve and discover. We did some work in the Rhondda. The ground was hard. On our second night we knew that something special was happening in another valley, where the river Taff flows to Cardiff.

Philip organized the first team. I was the pastor, singer and dreamer. Steve Cook was in charge of transport. John Tucker grew up in the valleys and was marvellous in helping us understand the history. The group consisted of mainly men who shared one room, and that's when we learned that Phillip snored like a troll.

We visited the old mining village, knocking on doors, saying we had come especially to meet them and inviting the young people to an event. Ever since I have loved stopping at the local store, buying a Western Mail and talking to people who had time to chat. That didn't happen so easily in Brighton.

So we went to Wales. To me the nation always had a sort of mythic quality to it, with the names of some towns that sound like they came form a novel by J.R.R. Tolkien. Every town seems to convey a history and to me a future.

Wales. The name itself stirred my soul. Rugby. Singing. Revival. Coal miners. Valleys and hills, rivers and seaside, and a unique language that those who are able converse in feel deep pride. Those that cannot are proud of the few words and phrases that we have picked up and of course the words to the greatest anthem of all.

Our first impression of the valleys was that it seemed to be "back in time". Few people used to go to actually visit the valleys as such. In fact were it not for the rich coal seams, I imagine that the population would have remained thin on the ground, in what is an area that is at times hard to access, though very beautiful. At one time tens of thousands of men were a mile deep under the earth, mining. Conditions were tough. Days were long. The wages were low but the sense of community high. The history is rich and it is said to be a proud history. Then the industry unravelled. Governments were brought down in the 70's over the issue and the world watched the Miners Strike of 1984. The decline continued. It was the end. I imagine that today it would be almost impossible to create safe enough working conditions to begin such an industry. But men laboured for decades under ground for hours on end. There were strong families and community.

Often it would take a miner an whole hour, once
underground, to ride or walk to where work began.
Then a long ride and climb back to the surface. Then
often a long walk home. The miners often walked back
along the road not the pavement. Then home to a miners
cottage. Two rooms up and two rooms down. A coal fire
and a tin bath drawn patiently for the need to scrub the
coal dust off the body until clean and sore.

This is why men had to organise themselves to stand
against bosses that often had no care for an ordinary
family's condition.

The number of workers had fallen after the highs
of the 1920's. As demand rose and then fell so numbers
were cut. Unions were powerful. Politics trumped the
spiritual life.

As the last of the mines were dying, the hills and
valleys were turning green again. The beauty increased,
while the social issues began to worsen with the lack of
jobs.
We found that we were treading where
unemployment and welfare or disability allowance was
the norm. Poverty was high. Addiction was rampant. In
one village a young man was pointed out to me who
had set himself on fire because of drugs. Teen pregnancy
was not unusual, nor was it highly unusual even to meet
a grandmother in her twenties. Manhood was
undermined. There was a cynicism towards hope. The
valleys of Wales were not the whole story of Wales, but
it became a part of our story.

It all began with Dave and Jean. We met them on our first mission, and they still today very dear friends and life-time partner.

I remember asking some young lads in the street on our first weekend,
"Do your like rugby?"
"Na".
"Do you like football."
"Yeh". But the "Yeh" was said with the same lifeless tone as "Na". The boredom was wretched.

"There's nothing to do" was the cry. Of course every generation has said that sometime, but to be fair there was not a great deal going on. Populations had declined dramatically. For instance Abertillery used to have 35,000 in population, three cinemas, working men's clubs, and department stores. Now there are only 7,000 and the big attractions closed down. Boredom was a huge factor. Wales were less successful at sports at the time. And there were no jobs.

Years later I walked with my friend Rich Terry in Troederhiw, we met a man called Malcolm. He was grateful for us being there. But he advised us, "it's all gone".

He meant that spiritually and economically there was no point even hoping. But we were caught up with this place already and came with an optimism that defied what we could see.

We noticed that there was not a great deal of warmth towards any kind of church activity. This has completely changed years later. We were outsiders, but our first night in Troederhiw was incredibly effective in connecting with young people. About 70 showed up. We only had about two hours to announce that we were even doing anything. We presented the gospel and several responded. From this night on, Jean and Dave started a youth work which they carried on for the best part of two decades.

The young people need this kind of thing. Many years later in 2015 we met a young business woman in Merthyr called Amy who went to their club and she was glad for us to pray for her.

At the time it seemed that there were plenty of anti-church folks. The church culture had often lacked joy and some seemed to value the pipe organ more than worship and the gospel. This had put several generations off,

"Boring", and "full of hypocrites"

But we saw that from about 12 years old or under, the story of the gospel was largely fresh. It was a new story and there was no negativity.

Twenty years later an entire generation are warmer than ever to the message. One day, in Blackwood 2013, I talked to a couple in a coffee shop. The dad was called Rhys, aged about 25, and he also named his son Rhys. He was amazed that I was Rhys. I had just asked him how to get to a place which means "valley", the Welsh word is Cwm.

He asked why would I go there? I said that it was a prompting. He asked me to explain what a prompting was.

He was bowled over why we were there and he thought it was brilliant. He asked if I could "christen" Rhys there and then. I called over Phillip and the current Senior Pastor of Holland Road David Treneer, a Cambridge University graduate. We explained what a dedication was and there and then, and with three minsters present, we dedicated Rhys in the street.

The younger folks in Wales didn't seem to have the cynicism to the gospel. It has been sweet to watch.

Back to Troederhiw, David Chilcott had seen people coming to Wales before and "try to take over", so we appreciated both his warmth and discernment towards us.

We now have ministered together for over 20 years. Do be discerning in life but don't be cynical, is a good premise. Or the word says it better,

Do not quench the Spirit. Do not treat prophecies with contempt but test them all; hold on to what is good, reject every kind of evil.

1 Thessalonians 5:19-22

There is a balance.

We stayed through the weekend and even onto the Tuesday night where Wales played Italy in a narrow win for Wales, after a poor start. Nigel Davies went over in the corner in the half empty old stadium, that only had three years of life left. His son now plays for Wales.

I continued to watch Wales play about once a year. A marvellous new stadium was built for the 1999 World Cup. So Wales had to play in England.

The move to Wembley for two years meant that I saw the narrow defeat to South Africa with a dear South African friend Karel Brink. Only the brilliance of "Joost", and bizarrely a six minute delay with a streaker, turned the game away from Wales. They had lost their previous game in South Africa by an embarrassing amount. Joost died early in 2017. He was a believer.

Chapter Six
<u>Wembley 1989.</u>

I took Megan to the defeat to Ireland in 1999.
Louise and I saw Billy Graham preach at Wembley in
1989. There were 85,000 there and 6000 people
responded despite a cloud-burst.

Ten years later the team walked onto the pitch.
Craig Quinnell ran into the posts and they wobbled and
almost fell over. There was a punch-up in the first
minute. I mentioned the posts to Craig recently at a
chance meeting not long ago. He thought it was funny
that I remembered.

Wales lost, but a second half comeback sparked a
momentum that led to a record 11 matches won in a row
in 1999. Rob Howley was the captain. The most famous
of those wins v England was on April 11th 1999
although a marvelous win in Paris, a first ever victory
over South Africa and an away series win in Argentina
was a great achievement. For the only time since 1972 I
missed the England game and was literally sharing on
the platform for New Hope in Fayetteville Georgia for
the first time at both campuses. The things I remember!

Aberfan.

Jean Chilcott introduced us to Aberfan. When
she drove Megan and I there the weekend of a rugby
match, Jean began to whisper. In 1966 a landslide
destroyed the local primary school tragically killing 144
souls. 116 were children. The village is deep in the soul

of not just Wales but also Britain. The Queen was a shocked visitor to the disaster in 1966 and has often remembered and been kind to the area.

Jean Chilcott was one of the Salvation Army workers who went to help in 1966 at the disaster scene. She was 16. Dave had been at the school a few years before and knew many who had been there.

In 1996 Holland Road was able to lead a choir event to a packed house at the community centre that is adjacent to where the disaster struck. We have sent several prayer-teams over the years, visited the school children of today and believe that this tragedy no longer dominates the area. Healing has come in time. The New Hope choir is due to sing on the site, now the community center July 2017.

Tragedy can take us deeper into faith. As Peter said to Jesus, "Lord, to whom else can we go?

The recording artist and Dove Award nominee John Waller wrote the song God Reigns Here on the site of the tragedy. It is a song that offers hope.

I am eternally grateful to Phillip Deuk and Dave and Jean, for their partnership. From this point on Holland Road and New Hope were able to connect with as many as 56 towns and villages in the Welsh valleys.

To say "my Grandfather played for Wales" has been a story that helps connect the dots.

By 2002 we were going regularly to Wales and we were trusted by many. The response got warmer and warmer as we did not just share words of encouragement but also practically.

We cleared a church-yard in Miskin, painted a school and helped residents in Gelli Deg, did murals in

Pontypridd and in the school at Troederhiw, installed a bathroom in Merthyr, transformed community rooms for Cwmammon, cleared a ton of rubbish on the wonderfully named Bogey Road, and painted another school in the Gurnos and a new community centre that houses a new church. My wife Louise led a community action team to create a pretty garden in Merthyr.

During this time new relationships were built. Dave and Jean connected us to more pastors in Merthyr. We discovered that this was where the Welsh revival first stuttered in 1905. The Rev Peter Price of Dowlais attacked Evan Roberts in Western Mail, while Evan was staying in Troederhiw. Dave showed me where Evan stayed and told of how the crowds loved him dearly. While exhausted the critics wounded Evan. Disunity occurred. This can be a national pastime.

In this same area we had the privilege of seeing pastors united. A prayer breakfast began. I don't know if it was through us, with us or despite us, but we felt included in a spirit of unity. Andy Pitt has now become a key leader in Merthyr which really has been our base. He is a great leader and has a brilliant sense of humour. Andy has spoken for us in Atlanta.

Two key initiatives that Andy led, have been mirrored across the UK. First "Street Pastors" have noticeably helped behavior on the streets, and made the UK safer. The crime statistics in Merthyr at one time represented a 40% improvement. We could testify to Friday nights outside the Castle Hotel being significantly quieter and making lives easier.

Then CAP, or Christians Against Poverty, with food banks, and debt counseling has taken root in most towns. An entire generation are seeing churches serving and being a big part of life. The caring is genuine and the local churches provide a fine service. Prime Ministers have even boldly praised local churches for do what they do.

John Parkin, a big Newcastle soccer fan, lived on the challenging estate of Gelli Deg. He and his wife Angie became great partners as they led St Luke's a small Church of Wales work that didn't invite people to services, but breakfast, followed by singing, prayer and a practical talk. One day I visited John with our daughter Eleanor to watch the British Lions. John told us that the previous week, after playing soccer with some lads, they literally pelted John with stones. He said it was their way of saying "thank you"!

On the morning of the bombings of 7/7/2005 in London, we saw six people converted in one hour, each in a different home. We couldn't explain it. Perhaps it was the sense of trust, or the combination of everything, or the shock from the news, but we knew that it was not our hand that did this.

We visited more frequently. Many of our Brighton church members had now served in Wales. I am so grateful that Holland Road listened to a pastor's passion and went for it. Sometimes we went several weekends a year. We had worked in the Rhondda, Cynon and Taff Valleys. There were forays to the Vale of Glamorgan and Abergavenny, including well attended events.

Soon we would find ourselves the Castle Hotel, Merthyr Tydfil. Mr Keira the manager has been a fine host and a good friend to all whilst keen to strengthen his business!

It turns out that "the Castle" was a key gathering point in history. The 1831 uprising had reports of 10,000 gathering outside the hotel with magistrates and iron masters holed up in the hotel. Many were killed. We hoped to bring life. But some Friday nights years ago were pretty messy outside the hotel.

Our "man of peace" Andy Pitt pastor of Park Baptist enabled us to be based at High Street Baptist whilst we served not just Merthyr but several valleys. But another key catalyst was to come. We were about to all go to the next level.

Chapter Seven
Hove 1995.

Let me take you back to 1995. Rich Terry flew in not on Concorde, but on a Delta flight to Gatwick airport to Atlanta, the busiest airport in the world. Rich was a veteran of the first Gulf war, but now an international pilot and a member at New Hope. Today he is Director of Line Operations of the world's largest airline!

He visited Holland Road, Hove one evening. We chatted for a while, and had a great connection. You never know when you are going to meet a key friend or influencer in your life. But Rich has become such.

Over the next couple of years we became firm friends, talked often in the phone, and eventually each time he flew over the would stay with our family. I don't think we could have made it to the USA had it not been for the cultural insight Rich gave us.

In 1998 Rich brought John Avant the pastor of New Hope then to visit us. John was a keen student of the Welsh Revival.

By 1999 Rich was the missions minister of New Hope and brought over 100 members of his church to Brighton all at once.

We had two girls Megan and Eleanor, with one on the way. Rich and his wife Vicky both had been to stay before, but this time Louise was expecting in just three weeks time. The baby was to be born at home in what is called the Church "Manse".

On the biggest day of the mission in Hove, Louise went into labour. Rich and Vicky were in the house. Within 45 minutes Sarah was born on the 4th July. Megan and Eleanor were delighted and Rich and Vicki have been like family to us all, ever since. They held Sarah when she was only minutes old.

John Avant was speaking for me in church that day anyway, so I had the morning off, holding new-born Sarah whilst Louise slept. I remember feeling much gratitude that day for so much. A defining moment. We loved each other, loved Hove, loved Wales. What more was there?

There were 100 New Hope members being put-up in Holland Road members homes, a feat not to be under-estimated. Friendships have endured ever since.

This repeated three years over. It had a big impact in Hove. We had rock concerts, choir events, and many visits to schools. New Hope members give up their vacations and the expense of the visit to serve in the UK.

When the terrorist attacks hit USA on 11th September 2001 or "9/11", the first thing I did was to call Rich. Airline travel has not been the same since and our world sees to be in a tough spot.

By 2002 Rich now as honorary missions leader felt that New Hope was not as effective in Brighton and Hove as the earlier days. Had we run our course? This may have been the end of the partnership. We prayed. They were unsettling weeks. But I suggested that Wales had a huge need.

Ever since then Holland Road have partnered together in Wales. We celebrated 20 years of these trips in November 2014. It has strengthened since then if anything. The first Welsh trip combined was a 20/20 trip: 20 from each Church for a week in Wales. We have been hosted very well by High Street Baptist Merthyr where we set up office. We have often had 70-100 people at a time on the trip. I have gone always at least twice in the year sometimes three times. Many from New Hope have been 10,12, and even 14 times.

People often ask, "what do you do in Wales?" Well, we just show up first of all. And we listen and love as best we can. We always keep the message simple. I'll summarize my message:

1. Wales is beautiful. Because only a supreme designer can create it.

2. Wales is also broken. The Bible tells us that mankind turned his back on God.

3. Wales is loved. I often quote the movie *The Help*, "You is Special...you is important!" The love is shown by the cross of Jesus.

4. Wales can be remade through faith in Jesus and following Him.

This message is communicated in so many ways. The specialness of each person can be seen in our Beauty days. The Gurnos estate once known as one of the worst in Europe has been served with say Megan cutting hair, chatting away kindly and then taking photos that we print out and send people home with. Or a visit to a care home says it all.

The visits to scores of schools is full of this message of renewal and hope. We have been in prisons, and church halls, coffee shops, churches, community centres and even rugby clubs! We have been up hills. Usually for the team photo. Once a prayer walk in 1994 got to a steep precipice at the top of the Rhonda. I have been in the snow and a heatwave in the Castle Hotel was stifling.

We have eaten a lot of quiche and Welsh cakes. The curries are always a special treat. Our day trips have included Caerphilly Castle and Abergavenney and singing at my mum's a wedding back in Teignmouth, the first time that New Hope, Holland Road, Wales and Teignmouth met, in part, together. At Cardiff Castle we saw the World Cup.

We have had days off afterwards many time in London, Brighton, Oxford, Cambridge, The Cotswolds, Stratford upon Avon, the home of Shakespeare, Salisbury and Bath. Perhaps we would not have seen these places had we not left. We have not yet seen Highclere Castle or rather Downton Abbey.

In London we have seen a Prime Minister announced. Once President Jimmy Carter was on our plane and so we have all shaken hands with a President of the USA.

We have "connect teams" all over the community inviting people to the choir events. We feel like we have tried everything! But I don't believe that we have ever been accused of being rude or pushy. And we never did take anything over. We never compromised our amateur status!

The tech teams work very hard. As do the kitchen team.

The team always gives a special shout out to Clarke Dailey and the tech team and Miss Linda our Cook.

Morning devotions at High Street, Merthyr unite the team. The Holland Road Team are brilliant. To see old friends stirs everybody. Increasingly the local pastors and churches supply all the minibuses and pull their weight considerably

We have visited thousands of children in schools and were grateful to teachers who sensitively allowed us in, knowing that a rich vein of a certain tradition of spirituality was not only part of Welsh history but still valuable.

We have visited many senior care homes, always hugely appreciated.

We visit people's homes and we were welcomed more and more as people knew that we were coming and trusted us.

We pray for people. We encourage the churches and eat more Welsh cakes and we are encouraged ourselves.

Things began to change. For a couple of years we brought fairly well-known bands in the USA like Two Bare Feet and Matt Papa. But it was hard to communicate how good they were til it was often too late.

Our choirs would only get modest crowds at first also. But as we found a more contemporary genre, as the 100th anniversary of the Welsh revival raised expectations, and as trust increased, we began to see larger crowds.

At core we presented the gospel especially with music.

Wales had a great history in this. But we began to find a niche that helped us bring something unique: Gospel music.

It just so happened that a few fresh soloist came to New Hope who are remarkable singers. Thousands have heard Sonya Knight, Toni Byrd and Jonee and Brendon Blair in Wales. The songs Send it on Down, God will Open the Windows and Thou oh Lord brought the house down. Recording artists John Waller, Drakeford, Matt Papa and gospel star Canton Jones have been on the team to Wales.

I have loved having our family with us. Louise has been marvellous enabling each of our girls to do a full week's mission at least 12 times each. I always introduce the family at the choir performances.

People left those nights vibrant. It seemed to spill out into the streets.

We have performed perhaps 95 choir concerts. We have got used to full houses. We have partnered with the Dowlais male voice choir, Garin Jenkins and Dai Morris. Emyr Lewis joined us one night as his son Jacob sang for us in Welsh. We have often joined with schools. One night in Neath I met Ron Waldron, former Welsh coach, watching his grandchildren. Whilst inviting people on the streets, I spotted Roland Phillips,

Welsh international and currently coach of the Wales
ladies team. He was surprised that I would know him.
Of course I said, you were excellent in the 1988 triple
crown. This unusual memory that I have has opened a
few doors. I think that rugby helps me remember the
events of my life. Apparently we all use reference points
to remember things. My thought processes may have
been affected by the five nations 1972!

I also popped into the Gnoll, home of Neath RFC
with John Conrad our Music and Missions Minister and
imagined Grandpa playing there for Swansea or Bristol.
Grandpa said that a visit to Pontypool was always
tough, because they would soak the leather ball in the
bath, to make it impossible for him to drop a goal over
the bar.

Things really changed in November 2004. Megan
and I did get to meet Sir Gareth Edwards and Gerald
Davies before a match. I expected us to win despite New
Zealand having some of the greatest players of all-time
in Ritchie McCaw and Dan Carter.

We saw Wales lose by a point. Wales were
becoming a force again. When the final whistle went the
NZ players seemed to collapse of the floor. Wales should
have won a famous game.

But 2004 was a shift not just for Wales but the
Stenners. By that year, the work in Wales was a decade
old with Holland Road and New Hope now having a
long term commitment to Wales. John Avant the senior
pastor had keenly supported the venture. He did his
Ph.D on the 1904-5 revival. Rich and I shared the
leadership with Phillip Deuk the key builder of the

partnerships with many Churches. He has served Wales and I would give him an OBE.

That November I was still pastor at Holland Road. I had outlived most of my critics after 12 years! We loved the Church. We lived 400 yards from the seafront and 600 yards from Sir Paul McCartney, who I had met already. And we were alive in Wales. I loved walking or running in the seafront everyday.

On a trip with us, John Avant told me that he was praying about leaving New Hope. The Church with 6000 members then, had had some struggles. I remember thinking that I would never want to swap with him.

That Christmas Day I went up to my study and prayed that John would not leave New Hope. In fact I was the main voice in John's life saying "don't go."

Two weeks later, my best senior pastor-friend Peter Brooks announced he was leaving the largest church in Brighton to take over a tiny church in Sydney. On the same day John announced to New Hope that he was a taking a denominational post. This was unsettling to me. I had felt led to lay down the leadership of a network of pastors in Brighton and Hove that I had been chairing for seven years. But I assumed that we would carry on in Hove for many years.

2005

It all changed in 2005. For the first time in a few years John Avant was not with us. So I became the main speaker at the choir events. Ever since 2001 our dear friends John and Donna Conrad became like glue for the missions. Each year John made the choir better. In recent years we have had recording artists as soloists including Grammy nominated Canton Jones who 2014 had his debut Number one on Billboard. John is a great leader, and administrative genius with a mystics heart!

July 2005 was seismic for us. We brought the choir again to Wales and connected we estimated with about 10,000 in the three main valleys through schools, concerts, and community projects.

I spoke in the July evenings of 2005 with a new freedom. That I could say "My Grandpa played for Wales" always gets a hearing. My passion for the Welsh revival always spilled out. I felt the congregations could be addressed as one. There was always unity. I gave my testimony and many responded to the message.

Back in America the "Pastor Search Team" was a slow process for New Hope. Over 100 "resumes" had been read. It was summer and the team would not be able to meet for a few weeks.

Rich told me that "some folks in the choir are putting your name forward".

This actually happened. We were shocked, but could not deny that something was stirring. To move even further away for Wales would not make human sense with all the progress being made. Our team in Hove was young. July 2005 was a huge success, the crowds were building, and churches encouraged.

But the call to meet the Search Team came. We travelled over at short notice, I spoke on the platform at both campuses at New Hope six years since the last time at the same time that Wales fought back against England.

The crowds applauded the sermon. I assumed this happened all the time. But apparently this was unusual. New Hope seemed older and a more traditional congregation to Holland Road. And much larger. The culture was different. Would they understand our accent? Certainly we read the same Bible. I spoke on Colossians 3.

We had two long meetings with the Search Team. They were kind and the team still today contains some that I respect enormously. Mr Lester Bray has been a church member for over 75 years. Don Boykin is a great life coach to me and was a senior editor at the main Atlanta newspaper. He also took me to Augusta!

We were shocked that they offered me the role of Senior Pastor at New Hope. Randy Weaver called his wife Melody on her cell phone, as she drove us home after the team deliberated. Just as when we were married, and when we met Holland Road in similar circumstances, there was a thunderstorm. Georgia style.

Things move slower for Brits. I thanked Randy Weaver chair of the Search Team, and said we would let him know in two weeks after praying though with our leaders in Hove. It was quite amazing how none of us wanted to be parted in Brighton. But all of us saw God's hand.

The day before we were to tell Sarah, now six years old about the move, remarkably she asked me if we would ever move to America near Rich and Vicki! We saw the way prepared for us all.

Our last Sunday was a tearful parting. Friends like Sean and Neil Avard, John Elbourne and Mike Bray stayed til we drove home, along with David Treneer, Adam Dracott, Tim Symonds, Phillip Deuk and many others.

We wept as we left 18, Coleman Ave Hove with Keith Charman our driver.

We did know that we would be back in July 2006 to serve Holland Road and of course Wales. It was a great comfort to move to a church where literally hundreds had visited us in the UK. But we have been given many more dear friends. New Hope is an incredible church.

New Hope.

So we moved to Atlanta Georgia. We had so much to learn. George W Bush said when interviewed by Irish American, David Feherty,

"You have shown that you can be proud of your heritage and still be a great American".

We came because of a call. But we believed that we should be who we are, be ourselves and adapt where necessary. Nonetheless with girls aged 6,12 and 14 we figured that this move was huge and probably permanent. We are always at the mercy of a call. But we tried to put down roots, bought a house and eventually became dual citizens. When in Rome. Though not Rome, Georgia!

Leaving on a jet plane.

It was time to leave the U.K. The five of us stood in a tight circle and wept in the hallway. Louise was a rock, but myself and the three girls were unable to speak. Keith our neighbour and a friend was driving us to the airport. We handed him the keys to our house where we had lived for thirteen years, where Eleanor and Sarah were born, just 400 yards from the seafront in Brighton, and 600 yards from Sir Paul McCartney's house!

We loved it here. We had been very happy. We also handed in the keys to my office at Holland Road Baptist Church where I had been Senior Pastor for all that time. The night before we said goodbye to our friends who had been family to us. We all wept as we left the large chapel where I had preached over a thousand times. On Sunday nights after the service, and the last visitor had left, the girls and I always sprinted to the car laughing. This time we walked slowly, reluctantly, waving and looking in effect for the last time at our world that was our home. This had been our happy life, with some troubles of course. But we didn't really want it to end. The decision was right but it can sometimes hurt that one has to <u>decide</u> to leave what and who is precious. It is easy to be misunderstood.

My friend Neil was bothered that I was weeping so much that night. He reminded me that God had led us. I had no doubt about that. Louise, myself and the girls, and even six year-old Sarah had clear guidance. The leaders at Holland Road, and many in the Church had also seen us prepared for this. We were all sure that the Lord would provide and fulfill His purposes. But we knew this was a far, far and away goodbye. Though "leaving on a jet plane", not on the Mayflower, the impact on our family would be a whole new world, with no way back.

Time to leave. We boarded at Gatwick Airport, London. Wept some more. Prayed silently as we did an ocean crossing that has become our road most traveled by. Watched a movie. Dozed. Nine hours later we came up the escalators at the world's busiest airport, holding hands.

A hundred people greeted and hugged us. A clown's firetruck parked outside with clowns loading our luggage while police officers stared. Our subdivision was crammed with cars and hundreds were in our house when we arrived to southern hospitality. Every room had been decorated by New Hope. We still are thankful.

We spoke to everyone and thanked them. For the next weeks we were in a whirlwind of change, as I learned about being one church in two locations, leading a large staff, dealing with a church cash shortage, trying to get a social security number, figuring out healthcare, how to pump gas, drive on the right side of the road and getting a handle on the local customs, shaking thousands of hands at the Christmas events, and eating our first Chick-Fil-A personally delivered by Dan Cathy the President of the company! We had to start all over. And we wondered who we were: British or American? Do we say water like "War-ter" or "Wahder"?

But we knew that we were on the journey that began at conversion and never really ends. People were so kind and told us to keep our accent.

There is the occasional word of course that we mutually misunderstand but I like to say that our girls are bi-lingual!

The girls had to change a lot. They caught a yellow school bus instead of walking to school in 5 minutes. Each was at a different school due to the ages. Not everyone understood that they had spent as long as ten years learning a history that was discounted in the USA where Georgia and the USA is the centre of the earth, as every nation believes itself to be.

And Maths is actually Math.
And centre is center etc.
And we all actually say potato the same. Though not tomato.

But New Hope is a loving place. The vast majority were very kind and supportive, some of the best people one could know. All with a southern drawl.

New Hope has become a very diverse church and so the gospel choir that goes to Wales reflects that. Our city has had a checkered history but we hope to be part of bridging the gap. Our Church has an incredible Christmas production attended by 12,000. And an alternative to Halloween draws thousands more.

There is a spirit of adventure that has taken us to innovation and daring. We go to most continents. But we remain rooted to the core of our faith and community.

And strangely despite moving to Georgia, the Welsh mission has grown and so has the connection with rugby

We have had some glorious nights in Merthry, Abertillery, Ebbw Vale, Cwmanmon, Aberammon, Ynysybwl, Rhigos, Dowlais, Hirwaun, Ferndale, Porth, Pontyclun, Trecynon, Mountain Ash, Pontypridd, Blackwood, Abergavenny, Troederhiw, and Aberfan.

One of the most memorable was in Neath. St David's Church, a large centrally located building was jam-packed. There were 100 people stood outside in the rain. Estimates varied from 650-800 there. We do know that 58 people responded to the gospel and handed in a decision card. David Trenner told me that several stayed all the way through, standing in the rain, and many were converted from there. There was great joy. I went to the main door and people were thrilled from the night. One man introduced himself as 88 years old, Vivian Williams. He said " I gave my heart to the Lord". A lady had his arm and said
"He's going to come with me to the Salvation Army!"

Great joy. What a night. We had two other big nights in Neath.

Pastor Chris of Ramoth, Hirwaun told us that our visit there was the largest attendance in his church since the 1904 revival! I told the packed house that night that on Christmas Eve 1904 Evan Roberts was preaching in Hirwaun. The night before he had been in Treherbert. The people walked all the way "up the Rhigos" to the top of the Rhondda and down the hill to Hirwaun, with snow on the ground, to hear Evan. Several miles, in snow, on Christmas Eve. How easily we give up today!

On 2015, 72 responded in one evening in Abertillery with a crowd for more than 500. The follow up always depended on the quality of the ministry in each place. We must always be ready.

2016 I claim three glory nights in Trecynon, Merthyr and Ebbw Vale. 42 responded in one evening in Trecynon.

Our message has been one of encouragement. It is a beautiful land with plenty of brokenness that Christ and his loving people can heal. But there's some more rugby.

In 1999 we won a competition for tickets to the Opening Ceremony of the World Cup. Megan, now aged eight, and I were guests at the Jury's Hotel, Cardiff and we had breakfast with the referees including Derek Bevan, Clive Norling and Jim Fleming. Paddy O'Brien I believe refereed the opening game v Argentina. He gave us a New Zealand fern-badge. We had lunch with Jonathan Davies who was kind to Megan and also the Aussie great Michael Linagh. Another number 10.

Throughout the day we chatted with the warm and amiable Clive Rowlands, Brian Price, and Robert Jones. We were sitting by the commentary box, just like Bristol days, in this new marvelous stadium that was frankly still being fixed up. The P.A. was terrible, but the Opening Ceremony incredible. We had Max Boyce, Shirley Bassey, Catatonia, Michael Ball, and a mass choir singing the hymns.

The game was almost an anticlimax but Wales won. Garin Jenkins famously slid along the touch-line, leaving a huge gouge on the pitch, which would still be there, had they not taken the pitch away so often.

Garin remarkably kept the ball alive for Colin Charvis to finish off the move with a try. I lifted Megan in the air so she could see but I learned not to do so anymore! Mark Taylor made the game fairly safe with a later score. I finally spent an hour with Mark recently.

All our girls cheer for Wales, as does all of New Hope. This was not the case at Holland Road where I learned to be quiet when England lost!

At the end of the World Cup Opening Ceremony, we spoke for a while to Gwyn Jones who had been virtually paralysed two weeks after we saw him lead Wales v New Zealand at Wembley in 1997. The day Gwyn broke his neck, Garin leaped into the crowd where his own Father had a heart attack. Garin went to hospital with his Father. Garin was still in his "old-school" Swansea shirt.

Two years on Gwyn walked slowly with walking sticks. We assured him of our prayers. Usually I tell international players that I pray for them, which I do, and I am proud of them. On match day I pray for each by name. We all need encouragement.

As a family we came all the way to Cardiff to Brighton for the 2005 Grand Slam celebration. The girls were desperate to get close to the players but news was that the Prince of Wales would be there and security would be high. So we had to see Shane Williams, Gavin Henson and Ryan Jones at a distance. Though Megan has travelled with me the most, it matters to all the girls that Wales do well. They all have Grog figurines. Google it if you don't know what it is. Eleanor's was Shane Williams and Sarah's was Rhys Williams. Megan has Gethin Jenkins and George North who we have met

more than once. Eleanor is the only one of the girls to
see the British Lions.

I won't mention every game we attended. But
our last game whilst living in the UK was Wales, in a
poor game v Fiji, where a late Nicky Robinson drop goal
saved the day. We were reluctant to leave the stadium
that had been a special place to us the last few years.

It was time to drive back to Brighton. We walked
slowly away, always the last to leave, just like church,
when we saw Garin Jenkins doing an interview. We
waited and said hello and said that we were leaving in
two weeks. We never thought that six years later he,
Helen, Lowri, and current Cardiff Blues and World Cup
U20 finalist Owen, would stay with us here in Atlanta.
Garin was the last Welshman we spoke to before leaving
our old life behind. We didn't realize how amazing that
was until
later.

Chapter Eight
Chicago 2009.

So we were now in America...

New Hope accepted this new family and were so kind to us. I preach at our South Campus at the 9.15 service and travel 12 miles to the North Campus for the 10.55 service.

There is not really a church like it in the UK. So we were learning a new culture. We could see Wales games on rather poor quality computer feeds.

Our girls learnt to school in the USA.

In 2009, Megan graduated from high school. It's a tradition for the graduating seniors to go on a "senior trip". So I took Megan to Chicago to see Wales play an international against the USA. This turned out to be a remarkable day. We got to the ground where Neil Jenkins was kicking balls to Nicky Robinson and Dan Biggar. The ball bounced over Neil straight into my arms. I used my old scrum half skills and spun the ball back to Neil using the voice of Bill McLaren saying "pass to Neil Jenkins". Neil got it and laughed. We have met a few times since. He is a class act.

The British Lions were touring South Africa at the time but it was still a strong Welsh team. A pleasant conversation with Sonny Parker helped us stay in touch on Twitter. He remembers me as the one who remembers facts and statistics about Wales. I have been grateful for the friendship on-line with other players like

Paul Turner a similar mercurial fly half who may have played more for Wales. He was brilliant v England in 1989.

At the end of the game we basically spent the evening with the entire team except Ryan Jones who was suffering from a concussion that famously ended his chance of being a late addition to the Lions. Concussion protocols have changed since then and Ryan would have been spared a long flight today. (It reminds me that when I was concussed playing for Teignmouth at fly half, that they just put me back to full-back!).

After a comfortable win for Wales, we were there for the awarding of caps, which you can imagine meant something to Megan and me. We were snapping away with our new devices called iPhones!

Carmarthen-born Dwayne Peel presented the caps, as a captain for the day and served with real class. I think it may have been his last game for Wales, which is quite baffling to many despite the powerful Mike Phillips accomplishing so much. Another Carmarthen boy in Bristol.

It was especially noticeable that current Wales Captain Sam Warburton received his cap as did also young Jonathan Davies, otherwise known as Foxy, after a pub his family owns. We had a good chat with Jonathan and I told him how much this Welsh cap meant. I could tell that Sam was going to be a leader. Not sure I thought he would have so many trophies by the age of 26. I have bumped into them both a few times. They both have a friendliness that is refreshing for such superstars.

Jonathan also scored two tries that day. This was a sweet time for Megan and I. Having emmigrated we promised her that we could still see some rugby. A lot of people have enjoyed looking at the picture of her with Luke Charteris who stands at six foot 10. This would not be the last time with the Welsh team.

A few months later, on our annual leadership tour that builds the partnership with leaders, I met John Bullock. He and his family are dear to us. John is now in Africa. But half of John and Debbie's life-ministry has been devoted to Wales. John spoke for us at New Hope and encouraged us that we would connect with millions of lives. We certainly have connected with hundreds of thousands and the impact of our members has national reach, and is another story.

The following summer John re-introduced us to Garin Jenkins. We met at the Vale of Glamorgan Resort, where John was a member. John was Garin's pastor. Garin's winsome personality, as well as his legendary status, playing 58 times for Wales, means he is very popular. No-one has started more games than Garin in his position. There are so many talking points with Garin: the last miner to play for Wales, the famous eye-gouge picture, throwing in the ball for Scott Gibbs try, winning 11 tests in a row, beating South Africa while they were World Champions, sent off in South Africa, after dinner speaker, BBC commentator, his son playing in a World Cup final, beating Australia 1991 World Champions again and scoring a try for Swansea; but everyone agrees that he is the most genuine and kind of men. His radio comments are outstanding. Rarely does a week go by without the Welsh national newspapers having a picture or reference to Garin.

Garin's meekness is not weakness. He has stayed in his home village and dotes on Helen, Owen, Lowri and his mother 300 yards away, who keeps her home almost as a museum to Garin! When Garin takes me around the area he always says, "Rhys's Grandfather played for Wales".

We went for a walk the first time we met and who should we bump into next but Neil Jenkins. It's amazing how these things happen. I told Neil, Wales' record points scoring fly half, about Grandpa and why I come to Wales.

We have had long chats since.

Garin became part of our Wales mission and has helped lead many men's nights, sometimes called beast-feasts, that encourage so many. It has been a thrill for Garin to bring along friends like Nigel Meek, Byron Hayward and Emyr Lewis.

After the New Zealand game in 2014 Garin, Megan and I were saying farewell in Cardiff, as we were leaving to go home. Thousands were piled into the city. We were saying final words when a man approached us. He said he had lost those he was traveling with, and asked if could he stand with us for a few minutes. The place was noisy and even a little intimidating. We invited him to join us. He discovered who we were and I asked if he would like us to pray with him. (Garin later told me that he was a man he recognized as a very able man). The man was thrilled. He was amazed.

"Of all the people I could have asked to help me I picked you!"
We were honoured and encouraged him to seek the Lord.

New Hope loved meeting Garin when he came to give his testimony one Sunday morning. This testimony is still available online and we inaugurated him as the first international member of our sports hall of fame.

Garin invited us to stay with him several times. Louise celebrates Helen's Welsh cakes as a true delicacy. Garin showed us where the pit used to be with a thousand men working there in his day. We have watched games together, in Cardiff. We watched the Lions beat Australia on TV in 2013 in Ynysybwl. Owen his son ate a huge number of poached eggs. Owen played in the Under 20's World Cup Final and is an experienced international sevens player. We have been Garin's guest in the Principality Stadium international lounge and had a picture with Sir Gareth Edwards!

When Garin and Helen stayed with us, I took him to my local Arnold Palmer-designed course. He didn't know that I played a bit. I birdied 6 of the first 10 holes and he was a bit shocked as he had found the water once or twice. After I coached him a little bit, Garin gave our family several rugby coaching sessions on our front lawn. He was "Shalk Burger" the South African and we were Wales in the World Cup. Garin has all his coaching badges and loves to do funny voices whilst he coaches! My girls loved it. Owen joined us a couple of days later and showed his range of rugby skills on the front lawn that helped him do what Garin has not: played in a world cup final!

At both the regions that Garin has coached, he helped several superstars emerge. He told me that once towards the end of an intense scrummaging session he said,

"Let's try something new. Let's try pushing!"

A number of rugby men have grown spiritually through his kindness and patience.

I was honoured when his local rugby club Ynysywbl RFC made me a member. We have since taken the choir to the club and also Garin and I shared an evening with Grammy award nominee Canton Jones and Megan and her husband Alex. I've enjoyed training with Garin at the club, as well as in my gym where Garin met our church member Lee Haney, Mr Olympia 8 times, beating the record of "Arnie".

One session Garin wanted to train at the Bwl or Bull, the ground of Ynysybwl. He said we should box. So I had to hit his hands, with pads for a minute or so. Then he was to hit my hands. He hit me so hard that my padded glove flew off and went 40 yards behind me. My shoulder had been tight and amazingly has felt better ever since! I still haven't the heart to tell Gar that I am two years older than him so maybe I should be his fitness coach!

There are many needs in the village of Ynysybwl, symbolic of the challenges in postindustrial Wales, but it's good to know that there are praying people in the village and a wonderful welcoming group at "the Bwl". I feel a sorry for the debt that the club has, from a former dispute, and hope that a kind benefactor could help them out.

Garin has sent encouragements to Fayetteville, Georgia more than once during games from the BBC Radio Wales commentary box on international days.

The postman knocks twice

The story of post-master Dave Chilcott, Troederhiw was key. But we stumbled across another one. About 2009, With two weeks to go to the annual big mission, a church wasn't able to be able to host an evening; so we ended up in Cwmammon the home of the band the Stereophonics.

This village is really the end of the line, but we love it. At short notice the choir were invited to song. We sang at Moriah church and have become great friends with Dale and Helen. Dale was postman and pastor. Most churches cannot afford a full-time pastor these days. Dale and Helen have been to our home several times and Dale really is a key regional leader along with Philipp and Andy Pitt. The first time we were there, the church was packed out, and Dale is now the church's first full time pastor in a long history. Holland Road did an incredible job refurbishing the church hall that has become a very cool coffee hub. Dale is thoroughly Welsh, cannot speak a word of Welsh, and gets lost outside the village. I have to tell him how to get around. But he is a great Welshman.

He is so unpretentious. Self deprecating people have a winsome way. The welcome from the hillsides has been so consistent over the years. Barely anyone has been jealous or overly suspicious. There is no reason to be jealous, because the success of the relationship is "how can we help you fulfill your mission?"

Chapter Nine
<u>Rhigos 2014</u>

Having a heart for Wales is quite a remarkable thing. I believe it comes through the Spirit for the "flesh" would have given up long ago.

In the summer of 2013 we were at the beach in Florida, five hours south of where we live. I love to read, and decided to read a few books on coal mining in the Welsh valleys!

At the same time, as I discovered books on Kindle, I was able to download a book I had always wanted to read, the autobiography of Dai Morris called Shadow.

I found myself on the beach in Florida transported in my mind to the village of Rhigos itself. We had often been very close to it, but it is a village that one doesn't naturally pass through. Hence it is has a unique warmth to it.

That glorious night in Hirwaun, two miles away was a fond memory. We frequently ascended to the top of the Rhondda, a favourite visiting spot, where we would overlook the Brecon Beacons and often take a team
photo. The village of Rhigos is below and closer still is the Tower Colliery, the last working underground mine in Wales. It stayed on my mind, and I would occasionally visit on GoogleEarth.

We were on our regular leadership visit, with Pastor David Treneer, Phillip Deuk, Mark Conrad, Ellis Daniel, who represent new churches, and John Conrad.

They are all witnesses to what took place. I had not shared the burden of Rhigos yet.

We were returning from a visit from Church on the Rise in Ebbw Vale, we had a spare two hours on our schedule. Then I shared this burden. Immediately on this grey overcast day, a brilliant sunbeam shone like a stage light over the area which we reckoned to be Rhigos. I have shown the photograph to others several times. When we arrived at the village, the rest of the team stayed on our small bus. I popped into the local store under the guise of buying a Western Mail. After I had bought it, I asked the lady in the store if Dai Morris ever popped in to shop.

She said "a couple of times a week". Knowing that our time was short, I told her to say that if he came in the next few minutes that "Rhys was up at the rugby club". I still didn't know even where it was.

We went up to the club, walked on the pitch, and I did a little video-recording for Mark for his church magazine. As I was talking, I suddenly noticed a man walking up the hill. It was Dai. The team had a great conversations with the great man. Phillip said to Dai,

"Rhys's grandpa played for Wales."

I told Dai Morris Grandpa's name, and we talked about Garin too. We had a word of prayer. We offered to come back and bring some music. Dai said that he would talk to the committee.

Now let's go forward eight months to a remarkable evening with a full house at the club, with

Canton Jones singing, Garin sharing, and yours truly sharing a word. It was a magnificent night.

Dai Morris stood up, thanked us for coming and presented me with a beautiful miner's lamp.

So within 11 months after being on the beach, reading a book about mining and Dai Morris, he was now giving me the miners lamp. This may not seem remarkable to some but I believe that it was with no human manipulation involved but it was all in the plan. Light shines in unexpected places. This was a very happy night in Rhigos.

This year we took the whole choir to another glorious night there.

When Megan and I visited Chicago in 2009 to watch Wales play the USA, we bumped into the Welsh Manager Alan Phillips in the elevator, or what I still call the lift.

I thanked him for what he has done for Welsh rugby. I was thinking of two grand slams in just three years. Alan was a little wary because he was probably thinking of two recent narrow defeats in 2009 to Ireland and France.

I reassured him that I was not messing about, but just wanted to thank him. I have noticed that it can be a national tenancy at times to discourage, rather than encourage, making public figures a little wary.

So that was the end of that conversation and all was well.

A few years later, I believe it was also 2013, we happened to have a conversation with the Welsh coaching group one evening. This time Warren Gatland was working for the British Lions, so we had a delightful time with Alan, Sean Edwards and Rob Howley. Of course I told them about Grandpa but also what we were doing in Wales. I recounted the conversation that we had in Chicago with Alan and he did remember.

So by Autumn 2014 I hoped for the opportunity to be able to see Owen Jenkins training at the Cardiff Blues set up at The Vale.

On arrival the entire Wales team walked past Megan and myself. We said "Hi" briefly to the boys, and let them carry on, not wanting to be a silly hanger-on. We then bumped into Alan Phillips who kindly remembered us. He then said "What are you doing next", and he invited us to training. We were suddenly in rugby-Heaven.

We followed his car through security and parked up above the pitch. As we parked Megan told me not to hit Jamie Roberts or Dan Lydiate!

It was cold that autumn afternoon so Alan gave his training fleece to help little Megan keep warm. We walked on the edge of the pitch. The squad of 35 players were starting to loosen up. The coaching staff were there, seven or eight photographers, a couple of interns, and us.

Alan, who doesn't suffer fools, shared his story, his philosophy of leadership and allowed us just to hang around with the team for almost three hours. We will keep it a secret what we saw of course! It was fairly clear who the team would be a few days later.

We were cold but loved seeing a world class sports team train. Everyone knew what they had to do.

The senior coach observed keenly and said little. He had picked a great team around him. It was like watching Wales play Wales A for a double game. It was perpetual motion.

George North and Alun Wynn Jones were a commanding presence. George is vivacious and Alun Wynn, as you might expect for a legendary second row, was towering.

We had some great conversations and watched a world-class set-up. George North charged up and down the touch-line and we could almost feel the ground shake. We watched many players who have achieved much. This is a fine team. I tried to encourage everyone and reminded Warren Gatland that we were virtually the same age. He commented that he had much more grey hair.

Megan said one of the funniest things as we were about to drive away from the small car park to leave, as the light turned dark. We had been chatting with the kickers at the end, even kicking spare balls to Dan Biggar and Neil Jenkins. But as we reluctantly put the car into reverse, Meg said,

"Don't run over Neil Jenkins or Leigh Halfpenny!"

I tried to give lots of encouragement to the team. I believed them capable of an upset against New Zealand and though they only came ten minutes short of this, leading 16-15, thankfully they beat South Africa the next week for only the second time.

I like to reassure them how much we appreciate them and we pray for them. These are words not always spoken. I do believe there is something about the Welsh spirit that still does have a sensitivity to spiritual things. My feeling is that this goes back to heritage that was born in the midst of the many revivals that have swept Wales.

Nonetheless I was so grateful to Alan for his hospitality, inviting us back to other days which we weren't able to fulfill, but making sure that we made it to the captains run at the Millennium Stadium.

At the captain's run there were a few spiritual conversations. Like church, we were the last to leave and ended up holding the team bus door open for the lads to get on. George North was the last on the bus. We blessed them all! Rob Howley said that he was sure we need help from above.

Now of course you can imagine that I told the Welsh manager Alan that my Grandpa played for Wales!

World Cup 2015

I travelled over to the Wales during the world cup to encourage the churches and to lead a prayer time with the growing number of former internationals who are now following the Lord. I had no tickets. I didn't want that to be a focus. We arrived a few days after Wales stunning 25-28 win over the hosts England.

The team had been shattered by injuries but the likes of Dan Biggar and Gareth Davies were still walking on air. Ever the professional set up, the unit had stopped celebrating and were getting ready for a powerful Fijian team. Wales won well.

I have been impressed with the Wales management and players. Everyone seems to know what they should be doing. There is hard work and yet a calmness in the set up. Sometimes Warren Garland watches attentively Sometimes he is in the thick of it.

It is a rare experience to watch a world class set-up this close. Wales could have won with World Cup in 2011. During the 2015 they became Number 2 in the world until a narrow defeat against South Africa. It could have easily been a win for Wales.

But my job was to encourage and to lead a prayer-time. I know that it encouraged those who were there. And several of the management seemed not unhappy that we were on the premises asking for help from above! In fact Warren Gatland said that we need all the help we can get.

Our prayer-time was in a room called Pendoylan. It was so encouraging to see five world class former players fellowshipping and unashamed.

I had some great conversations with many of the team over a few days. Some nearing the end of their time with Wales, chatted about the future. It was an honour to chat with many household names, and we even gave out Atlanta Braves baseball caps. All I did was unofficial. No chaplain has been appointed. I try to just serve and encourage.

My frequent visits to the UK now have less rugby games taken in, and more connection with rugby people. Friendships have deepened.

Byron Hayward invited me to a day with the Scarlets. Coach Wayne Pivac has made the Llanelli Scarlets the leading team in Wales and at the end if true season won a magnificent final in Ireland to become Pro12 Champions.

I went on "defence day" a few days before a huge game v Saracens the European Champions. I arrived and was greeted by the entire coaching staff: Wayne, Bryon, Stephen Jones and Ioan Cunningham. We had coffee and then it was planning the day. Byron gave me a tour of Parc Y Scarlets stadium and the gym. We bumped into
James "cubbi" Davies the Olympic silver medalist and his more capped brother Jon "Fox" Davies. (Their father owned the Fox and Hounds pub hence " Foxy" and little brother "cubbi", the Welsh for cub.)

Byron joked that Stephen Jones and himself had 106 caps between them. Byron only had two but did score at hat-trick of tries for his first cap and became the greatest points scorer of all time in Wales at top class level. Stephen kicked over 900 points for Wales.

The team meeting was very technical but the culture very humble and approachable. Stars like Liam Williams, Jon Davies who remembered previous chats, Scott Williams, Aaron Shingler, Gareth Davies and Jake Ball came up to say hello. All very humble. Rob Evans is hilarious.

Then it was training on the blustery training pitch. I watched for an hour with Neil Jenkins and Mark Taylor. If it wasn't so cold I would have asked for the three of us to run with the ball. Neil was the first man in the world to kick over 1000 points in internationals and is the national squad kicking coach. Then back for lunch. Stephen Jones asked me to sign my book " If in Doubt" as I gave one to several of the team. As I left, I handed one to Jake Ball who had a fine season to follow for

Wales. Ken Owens was also a great man. Carmarthen boy. And most recently has captained the British Lions!

I am sure that Grandpa would have been thrilled. I miss him, and writing this makes his memory even brighter.

2016 was another year of meeting with leaders and sending over a large team to the valleys. We saw more glory nights as the choir sang and many hearts were warmed.

The Wales football team got to the semi finals of Euro 2016. The country was excited. We adjusted the time of the choir for the semi finals, night and we still had a full house. We sang in Trecynon and Pontyclun for the first time.

January 2107 was a valuable time with 38 leaders in Wales.

As we arrived in the U.K. light snow was falling across the M4 corridor. We wondered as we struggled to connect to the satellite images whether we should stop before we got to Wales for the night.

So we called Andy Pitt. His strong voice called out

"Keep going, the way ahead is clear."

He was right. We arrived in the valleys to only a dusting of snow. But the word maybe meant far more. We will keep going, for the way ahead is clear

I have just returned home from our 2017 July trip. Jet-lagged but jubilant. We stayed at the Castle

Hotel, Merthyr Tydfil once more. The nights are quieter than ever. Crime and unruliness is down. The owner Mr Khera is dear friend to us and he values the business and friendship back. Costa Coffee in town has good business when we are in town!

We have devotions 500 yards away in High Street Baptist. Then the teams dispersion across the valleys.

We had 82 on the team. The three main churches become one with local Welsh churches. We shared the gospel with over 6500 people in schools and care homes, coffee shops for unplugged events, church halls for family events. The connect team intentionally goes to streets and homes, especially to publicize the choir but the conversations are always meaningful. Almost no-one is rude to us these days. This year a barren piece of land in Troederhiw was made into a quality garden for the community. We had a rich time in with the choir Ebbw Vale, Resolven, Cwmammon, Abertillery, Pontyclun and back to Merthyr. I said this year that many said that we should sing in a famous national venue like St David' Hall. But truly we are more than happy to be at the end of the line, in a packed-out chapel that was once built to house a joyous crowd and to proclaim the gospel message. We know of 189 who filled out a decision card at the choir events this year. Many more were encouraged and who knows how many planted acorns shall be oak trees in heaven?

I continue to be amazed each year at what is happening. In summer 2017 a nation-wide mission began with tremendous effects. Could something more be stirring?

Hiriathe

Wales is a wonderful place. "Beautiful" as only a Welsh lady can say. It is a land of hills, valleys, and castles and famous for mines, chapels, and pubs. The underground mines have gone, many chapels have closed and few are full. I think of daffodils running alongside the river Taff in Cardiff. I see sheep on the hillsides in the Brecon Beacons and hear singing, and more singing. And rugby. And buying Western Mail and a packet of pastilles in the local Spa. But above all passionate people who have embraced someone whose Grandpa played for Wales and allowed a choir to sing in the land of song and for scores of folks to be part of the community each year.

We are honoured to have served the churches, the schools and care homes, and the local leaders and welcoming pastors.

A glorious revival remembered across the world is a story often re-told. I tell the stories of the revival, often at New Hope, always in Wales, and I hope that in the next twenty years we will yet see a tenderness in the hearts of the people as we have seen on so many glorious nights in Wales.

That Grandpa told me that he played for Wales, gave me his cap, told me to be a brave boy, witnessed my baptism, and told me to do whatever I did with all my heart undoubtedly helped me along in life. So many other people, have encouraged me, with only a few who would resent us.

But the greatest influence is the true Bread of Heaven, from John's gospel chapter 6, the One who makes a Calon Lan or a pure heart.

I have a vision of Wales being alight with joy again. A true revival. And of course I do get very excited when we win a rugby game. But even those games are comparatively nothing. So much of life is temporary. But the Word endures forever.

I encourage you to believe in the maker and savior of Wales and pray for revival.

Final Word

I am now a Grandpa. When I think of how my Grandpa influenced me, I pray that I can be an encourager, a friend and a dreamer for the maker of the hills and the vales.

Acknowledgements

I am grateful for and to so many people. This is a story of a special work. It's core is a tribute to a grandfather, my Grandpa, Ronnie Morris, who was a brilliant sportsman, a Welsh rugby international fly half and a great encourager.

To remember him is to think of all my family, my Mum and Dad, my grandmother, my uncles John and David, and Auntie Liz, and my cousins especially Eloise, an incredible athlete herself.

Thanks to my brother Peter and sister Sophie who all feature in the story.

Above all thanks and love to my brilliant wife Louise who made our move to America work, is a wonderful wife, mother and "Grammy". She has been so many times to Wales. She leads the practical community projects in the day-time and has sung at least 90 times in the choir in Wales.

Our three girls, Megan, Eleanor and Sarah and our son-in -law Alex, married to Megan, and our granddaughter Brynlee are all one team and they have done much for Wales. They are my greatest encouragers. And each have such rare gifts.

Teignmouth. Thank you to our home town and former church in Devon in southwest of England for teaching me so much especially my pastor Ian Burley, who showed me a vision for Wales.

Holland Road, Hove. Thank you to the Church that could see the leading of the Spirit when their pastor said "let's go to Wales" in 1994. Even though we left in 2005, Holland Road have never stopped serving the principality and have kept the passion high. All would say that it simply would not have been possible without Phillip Deuk, David Treneer, Sean Avard and Mike Bray and so many others like Grahame and Margaret and Keith and Sheila.

Phillip Deuk has served for thousands of hours in Wales and led more people to the Lord than any person that I can think of. His tireless work for pastors and his courage to gently share that we all need God in our life is remarkable. He is one of my heroes. He backed my initial heart for Wales and has never given up.

To my dear church family, New Hope. A "chance" meeting with Rich Terry led to a lifetime friendship on whichever side of the Atlantic we lived. Rich and Vicki brought my predecessor John Avant over and it took the work to the next level. They led the trips for many years.

John and Donna Conrad's diligence and service has not only sustained but strengthened the ministry. John is famous for leading over one hundred concerts where he leaps up and down with such enthusiasm!

Ellis and Kerry Daniel have had a major impact involving extra churches like Turning Point, First Mansfield, Texas and now serving with New Hope.

Thanks to Mark and Deborah Conrad and Turning Point for your commitment to Wales.

Thanks to hundreds of folks who have paid their own way, given up vacations and served with the team. Some have been more than a dozen times this way and Wales is in your soul, as is New Hope and the world.

To the entire fellowship at both campuses that I serve, we love you so much and are committed to you. It amazes me that we can estimate that over 300 members have been over to Wales. Thanks for permitting me to tell a rugby story at least once a quarter!

There are quite a number who have been on a mission trip numerous times. At this final juncture New Hope is mourning for Larry Reeves, a veteran of 14 trips. He has just gone to be with the Lord, just two weeks after the most recent mission.
Larry first came with his remarkable wife Pat and they were together several times. Pat's death was a huge blow. But a retired Colonel, Larry soldiered on and travelled to Wales numerous times as a widower. He has brought three different family members over, and most recently, though finding the travel quite arduous, made a significant mark for yet another year. His story is typical of many like him. He loved to visit people door-to-door and in the street. He led our care homes team,

visited prisons and even sang in the choir, though he
never claimed to be our strongest singer!
Tributes came in thick and fast after he died July 2017
from USA of course but also from England and Wales.

There are many like Larry who led the way who have
stuck with Wales. Another example is Dean and Cherie
Cotton with the clown ministry, having been at least 11
times. Dan and Linda Groce, Lisa McDaniel, and of
course Rich and Vickie Terry, and John and Donna
Conrad have been too many times to count.

Singers like Sonya Knight, Brendon and Jonee Blair,
Tony Byrd, David Allen, Forest and Sandy Cloud have
been outstanding.

And then there are the Cooks: Miss Linda and Miss
Linda!

To the churches in Wales. You are who we serve. But
thank you that there is now greater co-operation across
the valleys.

We thank God first for Dave and Jean Chilcott who have
enjoyed seeing so many others join in. Andy Pitt is the
most outstanding leader and our first point of call but
we also express gratitude to Dale and Helen Thomas,
John and Angie Parkin, High Street Baptist Merthyr, Ian
and Jill Anderson, Andy and Jan Ladhams, John and
Debbie Bullock, Chris and Justine Bullock.

And some people need no second name.

Nigel, "G" and Stacey, Gwyn and Jill, and Stan.

In the world of Rugby. It is a thrill to be close friends to Garin Jenkins, Emyr Lewis, Bryon Hayward and Chris Jones. Thanks to all their spouses and children. Our prayer fellowship has been significant.

Additional thanks for such warmth from Dai Morris, Nigel Meek, Andries Pretorius, Alan Phillips, James Hook, Mike Phillips, Sonny Parker, Owen Jenkins, Wayne Pivac, Stephen Jones, Ioan Cunningham, Neil Jenkins, Rob Howley, Warren Gatland, Robin McBryde, Jon Davies, Dale "Chief" McIntosh, and Paul Turner.

Special thanks to my executive assistant Valencia Marie Rose and my kind guest editors Laura Treneer and Sophie Duffy.

Thank you for the book cover by Eleanor Stenner and the formatting by Sarah Stenner. All the family have played a big part.

And a special memory for Evan Roberts through whom came one of the greatest revivals of all-time.

Appendix

Greatest Welsh fly halfs.

Percy Bush
Billy Trew
Harry Bowcott
R.R.Morris
Cliff Jones
Willie Davies
Glyn Davies
Billy Cleaver
Carwyn James
Cliff Morgan
David Watkins
Barry John
Phil Bennett
Gareth Davies
Jonathan Davies
Paul Turner
Neil Jenkins
Stephen Jones
James Hook
Dan Biggar

58 Villages and Towns included in our story. (We may have missed some.)

Treorchy
Cwmparc
Gelli
Porth
Ystrad
Ferndale
Pentre
Ton Pentre

Pontypridd
Coedpenmaen
Hawthorne
Treharris

Hirwaun
Rhigos
Resolven
Abercynon
Ynysybwl
Penrhiwceiber
Miskin
Mountian Ash
Cwmammon
Aberdare
Abercwmboi
Aberammon
Trecynon
Fernhill

Hensol
Pontyclun
Penwaun
Treventhin

Methryr Tydfil
Dowlais
Gelli Deg
Morlais
Penydarren
Pant
Cefn
New Tredegar
Pontypool
Cwmbach

Heol Gerrig
Aberfan
Merthyr Vale
Troederhiw

Nelson
Cwm
Abertillerry
Ebbw Vale
Brynmawr
Waunlwyd
Blackwood

Abergavenny
Dinas Powys

Barry
Cardiff
Neath
Gorslas
Swansea

Bibliography.
Assorted programmers of Bristol RFC.

Bristol Football Club 75th anniversary 1888-1963

Bristol Football Club. (RFU) 1888-1945. Mark Hoskins and Dave Fox. 2000, Tempus, Stroud.

The Dawes Decade. David Parry Jones. 2005. Seren, Cardiff.

Evan Roberts. The Great Welsh Revivalist and His work. DM. Phillips, Marshall Bros, London 1906.

The Great Revival in Wales. S. B. Shaw. 1905. Christian Life books.

History of International Rugby records -1987. John Griffiths. Phoenix. London 1987.

Instrument of Revival: The Complete Life of Evan Roberts, 1878-1951. Brynmor Pierce Jones. Bridge Publishing, South Plainfield, NJ, 1995.

Jim Griffiths. Pages from Memory. J.M. Dent and Sons Ltd. London. 1969

Prince Gwyn. David Parry Jones. 1999. Seren, Cardiff.

Rugby Bristol Fashion. Chris Ducker 1988. Thanet Press, Margate.

The Swansea Story. Brinley E. Matthews. Swansea and Cricket and Football Club, 1967.

The Times Archives 1937
Quotes from Bristol Fashion

"Bristol soon found an outstanding replacement – Ronnie Morris, the Swansea and wales fly half, had just taken up residence in Bristol and soon, with his astounding pace of the mark, and crisp well-timed passes, was creating more tries for the consistent Sherman", p. 82

"Morris was an inspiration", p. 83

More from Rhys Stenner

If In Doubt, <u>Worthy Publishing, Nashville, 2016</u>
If In Doubt provocatively addresses the seven greatest
questions essential for a lifetime of secure faith.
If In Doubt covers the grand story of all time, from
creation to the forthcoming close of human history and
into eternity.

"Few leaders have the conviction and intellectual capital
to write a compelling book like this. Rhys Stenner does
and also exudes compassionate leadership with pastoral
care in helping others wrestle through the toughest
questions in life. Get this book. Share it with others. Let
this thinker stimulate your mind, will, and emotion to
live your life with living faith."
Dr. Ronnie Floyd

This challenging new book, *If in Doubt,* makes it possible
for us to navigate the turbulent seas of scholarship and
science as well as the storms of skepticism and
searching. This book is so well written, with real world
illustrations, hard-hitting facts, and interactive questions
throughout.
Dr Jay Strack

To follow up with Rhys

Twitter: @rhysstenner
Facebook: A Minute of Hope with Rhys Stenner
Instagram: rhysstenner

19036912R00074

Printed in Poland
by Amazon Fulfillment
Poland Sp. z o.o., Wrocław